AMÉRICA INVERTIDA

Mary Burritt Christiansen Poetry Series
Hilda Raz, SERIES EDITOR

The Mary Burritt Christiansen Poetry Series publishes two to four books a year that engage and give voice to the realities of living, working, and experiencing the West and the Border as places and as metaphors. The purpose of the series is to expand access to, and the audience for, quality poetry, both single volumes and anthologies, that can be used for general reading as well as in classrooms.

Mary Burritt Christiansen Poetry Series

Also available in the Mary Burritt Christiansen Poetry Series:

Untrussed: Poems by Christine Stewart-Nuñez
Family Resemblances: Poems by Carrie Shipers
The Woman Who Married a Bear: Poems by Tiffany Midge
Self-Portrait with Spurs and Sulfur: Poems by Casey Thayer
Crossing Over: Poems by Priscilla Long
Heresies: Poems by Orlando Ricardo Menes
Report to the Department of the Interior: Poems by Diane Glancy
The Sky Is Shooting Blue Arrows: Poems by Glenna Luschei
A Selected History of Her Heart: Poems by Carole Simmons Oles
The Arranged Marriage: Poems by Jehanne Dubrow

For additional titles in the Mary Burritt Christiansen Poetry Series, please visit unmpress.com.

AMÉRICA INVERTIDA

An Anthology of Emerging Uruguayan Poets

EDITED BY Jesse Lee Kercheval

University of New Mexico Press ✛ Albuquerque

© 2016 by the University of New Mexico Press
All rights reserved. Published 2016
Printed in the United States of America

Library of Congress Cataloging-in-Publication Data
Names: Kercheval, Jesse Lee, editor.
Title: América invertida : an anthology of emerging Uruguayan poets / edited by Jesse Lee Kercheval.
Description: Albuquerque : University of New Mexico Press, 2016. |
Series: Mary Burritt Christiansen Poetry Series | In English and Spanish.
Identifiers: LCCN 2015046961 (print) | LCCN 2016000502 (ebook) |
ISBN 9780826357250 (pbk. : alk. paper) | ISBN 9780826357267 (electronic)
Subjects: LCSH: Uruguayan poetry—21st century—Translations into English. |
Uruguayan poetry—21st century.
Classification: LCC PQ8516.5.E6 A64 2016 (print) | LCC PQ8516.5.E6 (ebook) |
DDC 861/.70809895—dc23
LC record available at http://lccn.loc.gov/2015046961

Cover illustration: painting by María Noel Silvera;
photograph by Amanda Taylor.
Composed in Melior LT Std 10.5/15

Contents

JESSE LEE KERCHEVAL
   América invertida: An Introduction   xi

MIGUEL AVERO, translation by Jona Colson
   Sea Breaking Open / Mar descascarado   2 / 3
   Waters / Aguas   4 / 5
   Argument / Argumento   6 / 7
   Like a Sheet / Como una lámina   8 / 9
   That Sea / Ese mar   10 / 11

MARTÍN BAREA MATTOS, translation by Mark Statman
   from *By Hour, by Day, by Month* /
      de *Por hora, por día, por mes*   14 / 20

HORACIO CAVALLO AND FRANCISCO TOMSICH,
   translation by Geoffrey Brock
   Hermes I / Hermes I   28 / 29
   Hermes V / Hermes V   30 / 31
   Icarus III / Ícaro III   32 / 33
   Icarus V / Ícaro V   34 / 35
   Games V / Juegos V   36 / 37

MARTÍN CERISOLA, translation by Keith Ekiss
   from *Something Naked* / de *Algo se desnuda*   40 / 43
   [It's there—in the fire.] /
      [Es allí, desde el fuego.]   46 / 48

LAURA CESARCO EGLIN, translation by Lauren Shapiro
   Downpour / Aguacero   52 / 53
   Agency / Agencia   54/ / 55
   If the Storm Can / Si la tormenta puede   56 / 57
   Pasta with Tomato Sauce /
      Tuco con una buena pasta   58 / 59
   Photogenic / Fotogénica   60 / 61

LAURA CHALAR, translation by Erica Mena
   avenida 18 de julio / por dieciocho   64 / 65
   Montevideo / Montevideo   66 / 68
   Helsinki / Helsinki   70 / 71
   Guest / Huésped   72 / 73
   Poligrillo / Poligrillo   74 / 75

ANDREA DURLACHER, translation by Anna Rosenwong
   [I'm not like other ladies:] /
      [No soy como otras damas:]   78 / 79
   Life Is as Much the Same as It Is Profane /
      La vida es tan mimísima como profana   80 / 81
   [I begged the clock] / [Yo le rogaba al reloj]   82 / 83
   [I left a trail like Hansel and Gretel's] /
      [Hice como el camino de Hansel y Gretel]   84 / 86

VICTORIA ESTOL, translation by Seth Michelson
   flesh and fingernail / carne y uña   90 / 91
   Airport / Aeropuerto   92 / 93

[Dearest,] / [Estimado:]	94 / 95
minefield / campo minado	96 / 97
[two guys and me] / [dos varones y yo]	98 / 99

JAVIER ETCHEVARREN, translation by Don Bogen

Glue / Pegamento	102 / 103
Punta Carretas / Punta Carretas	104 / 105
Lungs / Pulmones	106 / 107
The Despicable Man Watching TV / Hombre vil frente a la televisión	108 / 109
Garbage Dump / Basural	110 / 111

PAOLA GALLO, translation by Adam Giannelli

Words Like Knives / Palabras como cuchillos	114 / 115
The Kiss / El beso	116 / 117
I Smell of "Amber Parenthesis" / Huelo a "Ámbar Paréntesis"	118 / 119
The Wave / La ola	120 / 121
Written from the Cave of the Predator / Escrito desde la cueva del depredador	122 / 123

EL HOSKI (JOSÉ LUIS GADEA), translation by Kevin González

Silence / Silencio	126 / 127
Benedetti Is a Good Grampa / Benedetti es un abuelo bueno	128 / 129
On a Plane There Were / Iban en un avión	130 / 133

LEONARDO LESCI, translation by Christopher Schafenacker

Río de la Plata / Río de la Plata	138 / 140
Milonga–Folk-land / Milonga–Folk-land	142 / 144
river plate fresh meat company / river plate fresh meat company	146 / 147

Saltwater River / Río salado 148 / 149
Thalweg / Thalweg 150 / 151

AGUSTÍN LUCAS, translation by Jesse Lee Kercheval
Plaza de los Bomberos / Plaza de los bomberos 154 / 157
General Flores without Flowers /
   General sin flores 160 / 162
The Hour of the Birds / La hora de los pájaros 164 / 165
River Runs / Río va 166 / 167

ELISA MASTROMATTEO, translation by Orlando Ricardo Menes
As Simple as That / Tan simple como eso 170 / 171
Game / Juego 172 / 173
That / Eso 174 / 175
A Before / Un antes 176 / 177
Hideout / Escondite 178 / 179

ALEX PIPERNO, translation by Vicente Marcos López Abad
from *Sahara* / de *Sahara* 182 / 184
Colony / Colonia 186 / 189
from "the lovers" / de "los amantes" 192 / 193
from "ars poetica two" / de "ars poetica dos" 194 / 195

ALICIA PREZA, translation by Julia Leverone
Sacrilege / Sacrilegio 198 / 199
Déjà Vu / Deja vú 200 / 201
The Spell / El hechizo 202 / 204
Olivetti / Olivetti 206 / 207
Scaffolding / Entramado 208 / 209

SEBASTIÁN RIVERO, translation by Catherine Jagoe
No Name / N. N. 212 / 216
mud / barro 220 / 223

JUAN MANUEL SÁNCHEZ, translation by Cindy Schuster
　from *For the Seals* / de *Para las focas*　　　228 / 232
　[Across a sea of grassland they came] /
　　[Llegaron a través de un mar de pasturas]　　236 / 237

FABIÁN SEVERO, translation by Dan Bellm
　from *Night Up North* / de *Noite nu norte* /
　　Noche en el norte　　　　　　　　　　　　240 / 246

PAULA SIMONETTI, translation by Catherine Jagoe
　Isabel / Isabel　　　　　　　　　　　　　　　254 / 255
　Nelson / Nelson　　　　　　　　　　　　　　256 / 257
　Gisela / Gisela　　　　　　　　　　　　　　　258 / 259
　Ramón / Ramón　　　　　　　　　　　　　　260 / 261
　What the Sad Say / En la boca de los tristes　　262 / 263

KAREN WILD DÍAZ, translation by Ron Paul Salutsky
　Thread of Blood in the Sky /
　　Hilo de sangre en el cielo　　　　　　　　　266 / 268
　Shelter from the Sky / Protege del cielo　　　　270 / 271
　The Sky Knows No Walls /
　　El cielo no conoce las paredes　　　　　　　272 / 273
　A House without the Sky / Una casa sin cielo　274 / 275

Contributors　　　　　　　　　　　　　　　　277

AMÉRICA INVERTIDA

AN INTRODUCTION

Uruguay, with only 3.3 million people, is the smallest Spanish-speaking country in South America and is nestled—or squeezed—between its larger Spanish-speaking cultural "brother," Argentina, and giant Brazil. Uruguay is proud of producing a disproportionate number of world-class soccer players, a valid position for a country that hosted and won the first World Cup. But, as I discovered living there, Uruguay produces an equally high number of fine poets. The international prominence of Uruguayan poetry stretches from the Uruguayan-born Isidore Ducasse, the Comte de Lautréamont (1846–1870), whose book *Les chants de Maldoror* served as inspiration for the French surrealists, to Julio Herrera y Reissig (1875–1910), whose work became a crucial influence on Rubén Darío, Pablo Neruda, Octavio Paz, and César Vallejo; from such strong early women poets as Juana de Ibarbourou (1885–1979) and Delmira Agustini (1886–1914) to Mario Benedetti (1920–2009), who was an important part of the generation that brought Latin American writing to world prominence.

Indeed, in his song "Biromes y servilletas" ("Bic Pens and Napkins"), the Uruguayan poet Leo Maslíah pokes fun at Montevideo, the capital, where half the country's population lives, as the place where "there are poets, poets, poets" who "claim neither glories nor laurels, laurels, laurels" and only "write, write, write" on every piece of paper they can find. Maslíah does not exaggerate. On most nights in Montevideo, one can find poetry readings in venues ranging from the national library to neighborhood bars.

Although culture is centralized in the capital, the smaller towns of Colonia del Sacramento, Minas, Tacuarembó, Artigas, and Maldonado also have poetry events, often organized via Facebook and other social media. Poetry readings frequently feature a mix of the most senior, established poets, such as Jorge Arbeleche, Luis Bravo, Tatiana Oroño, Silvia Guerra, and Roberto Appratto, with younger poets, some still students.

However, until recently, Uruguayan poetry has been difficult to find in English translation. This is starting to change. The last few years have seen the publication of translations of Mario Benedetti, Marosa di Giorgio (1932–2004), and Circe Maia (1932–), as well as two anthologies, *Contemporary Uruguayan Poetry: A Bilingual Anthology* (Bucknell University Press, 2010) and *Hotel Lautréamont: Contemporary Poetry from Uruguay* (Shearsman Books, 2011). Between them, these anthologies include the work of twenty-three poets, most previously unavailable in English. However, as I read these anthologies I noticed that the youngest poet represented in *Hotel Lautréamont* was born in 1963, the youngest in *Contemporary Uruguayan Poetry* in 1957. I knew from my time in Uruguay there were amazing younger poets as well, so I set out to find a way get their work translated and published. The result is *América invertida: An Anthology of Emerging Uruguayan Poets*.

For the previous generation of Uruguayan poets in *Hotel Lautréamont* and *Contemporary Uruguayan Poetry*, the inescapable theme is the civil-military dictatorship from 1973 to 1985 that sent many Uruguayan leftists to prison or worse and many poets into exile. Uruguayans read poetry with this in mind. They look for a poem's date to decide if a word like *silence* carries a double-weighted meaning. With Circe Maia, the first Uruguayan poet whose work I translated, this is certainly a consideration. In 1972 police raided her home to arrest her husband, leaving Circe behind only because she was caring for their four-day-old daughter. Her husband was imprisoned for two years. Her poem "Por detrás de mi voz," with its refrain of "Listen, listen, another voice sings," could be read as a poem about the continued presence of ancestors. But set to music by Daniel Viglietti in 1978 as "Otra voz canta," it became a political anthem throughout Latin America, a call to hear the missing voices of those "disappeared" by military regimes in Argentina, Bolivia, Brazil, Chile, Paraguay, and Uruguay.

Several poems in *América invertida* also take up the theme of the dictatorship—but from the perspective of a new generation, one that views these events as childhood memories or history. Typical of these is Sebastián Rivero's poem "No Name" / "N. N.," where Rivero writes movingly of seeing body "bags on the beaches / of your childhood," only to question the memory, "*can you see them? / do you remember?*" But this new generation of Uruguayan poets has been raised in a postdictatorship Uruguay, in an era of democracy and boom-and-bust capitalism. In his poem "Punta Carretas," to embody this generational shift, Javier Etchevarren uses the irony of the transition of the infamous Punta Carretas prison, which once held Tupamaro guerillas, into an upscale shopping mall, as personal tragedy becomes partly forgotten history. Speaking from the point of view of an imaginary ex-prisoner, he writes, "the prison is a shopping center now / that boutique was my cell / its plate glass windows my bars."

The previous Uruguayan president, José Mujica, is an ex-Tupamaro, one who escaped from Punta Carretas prison. For the past two decades, Frente Amplio, his coalition of left-wing parties, has been in government, legalizing abortion, same-sex marriage, and marijuana. This moderate progressivism is the reality for the young poets. And, at times, they are restless with the older generation of writers and their politics. In their song "No somos latinos," the popular band El Cuarteto de Nos pokes fun at the leftist history text *Open Veins of Latin America* by Eduardo Galeano: "I read '*Open Veins*' / and discovered it was slop. / By page four I was asleep." This impatience is especially pronounced in some young poets' attitudes toward Mario Benedetti, probably the most popular poet of the previous generation. In his poem "Benedetti Is a Good Grampa" / "Benedetti es un abuelo bueno," El Hoski goes so far as to imagine him as the opposite of good: "Benedetti is a wise grandfather . . . / I would stroke his mustache / and suck on his dick / how great Benedetti was / the voice of the people / if only we could all be like him."

But most of all, the younger poets' work is a response, not to history, but to what it is like to live in Uruguay now. In the sequence of poems from his book *Para las focas / For the Seals*, Juan Manuel Sánchez takes on what he sees as the contemporary worship of money and capitalism in mock biblical language: "The boss is my shepherd / he leads me through / fertile valleys / of perpetual bonanza / spacious offices / and exclusive perks." Andrea Durlacher's poems spring from impatience with the expectations placed on women by society, with lines like "I'm not like other ladies: / the street soaks up my wanting" and "Lassie is a do-gooder dog. / I'm not." In "avenida 18 de julio" / "por dieciocho," Laura Chalar expresses another common theme of the young poets, restlessness to see the world. She imagines what it would be like if Walt Whitman walked through downtown Montevideo, "how he would sing of them and sing to them with the deep voice of a street prophet," while she imagines herself watching "it all with the love of someone who is bound to leave, someone who is already leaving."

Paula Simonetti, Agustín Lucas, and Fabián Severo, on the other hand, write about the poverty and marginalization that exist even in the newly prosperous contemporary Uruguay. Simonetti, who works with addicts, the homeless, and the mentally ill, writes poems that are intimate portraits of lives of poverty and abuse. In her poem "Isabel" the woman in the title lies "sleepless listening to others sleep / that room / the sound of lungs the wheezing / music of indigence in that room." In his prose poem "General Flores without Flowers" / "General sin flores" Lucas objectively but sympathetically chronicles the life of street people, "The transients sleep, children of the street, with one eye obviously open, the proprietors of the stairs and of the railing, of the glass, of the bottle, of the remains of noodles and the heels of bread." Fabián Severo—who has taken the highly unusual decision to write in

Portuñol, the dialect of the Uruguayan-Brazilian frontier—writes of the isolation of border towns like Artigas, where he grew up, and the lack of respect for their culture. In *Night Up North / Noite nu norte / Noche en el norte*, Severo stakes his claim for the frontier as literary territory, writing, "Before / I wanted to be from Uruguay. / Now / I want to be from here."

The poets in the anthology write about their subjects in a wide range of forms and styles: Horacio Cavallo and Francisco Tomsich compose sonnets, Agustín Lucas writes prose poems, Alex Piperno's poems move toward Language poetry. Alicia Preza's and Karen Wild Díaz's poems flirt with surrealism and El Hoski's, with spoken word poetry. Indeed, the poets have read widely and are influenced by an entire world of poetry. As you can see in the biographies at the end of the anthology, the poets list Uruguayan poets as influences but also Bukowski, Dickinson, Carver, Poe, and Pound as well as Baudelaire, Lorca, and Vallejo.

The title for *América invertida* is taken from the 1943 drawing of the continent upside-down by Joaquín Torres García, a work of art that is distinctly Uruguayan and one that every Uruguayan knows. Founding his art school, Taller del Sur, in Montevideo, Torres García said it is "the School of the South because . . . we now turn the map upside down, and then we have a true idea of our position, and not as the rest of the world wishes." Today, defining their art—their poetry—and its place in the world is just as important to young Uruguayan poets.

When I began editing *América invertida*, I approached the project as a poet who is also a translator. I went to night after night of poetry readings. I collected books and unpublished work, reading more than sixty poets before finally selecting the twenty-three Uruguayans born before 1975 who appear in the anthology. I was looking for quality, but also range—of subject matter, style, age. I wanted the anthology to fully represent this moment in Uruguayan poetry. Then I paired each Uruguayan poet with an American poet/translator. Poets translating other poets into English is a tradition with deep roots. From Robert Bly's seminal translations of

Neruda and Vallejo on, these intercultural exchanges have been crucial to the development of poetry in the United States, opening up our vision of what poetry *is*, not just in America, but in the Americas.

My other goal in pairing each poet with a poet/translator was the hope that lasting connections would be made, one that would open a dialogue among the poets. I am happy to say this often turned out to be true. Many translators translated more than the five poems for the anthology, and those poems, as well as poems from the anthology, have appeared in literary magazines and translation journals such as *American Poetry Review, Asymptote, Beltway Poetry Quarterly, Blue Lyra Review, The Collagist, Colorado Review, Copper Nickel, Diagram, Notre Dame Review, Palabras Errantes, Poetry, Prairie Schooner, spoKe, Tupelo Quarterly,* and *Words without Borders.* Already two books—*Bicho Bola* by Victoria Estol, translated by Seth Michelson as *Roly Poly* (Toad Press, 2014), and *Anti-ferule* (Toad Press, 2015) by Karen Wild Díaz, translated by Ron Paul Salutsky—have been published, and two more books are forthcoming. At least four other translators have plans to translate and publish books by their Uruguayan poets, and several of the Uruguayans are equally excited about translating the work of the Americans into Spanish. This is what I hoped to see. But the main fruit of this project has been this anthology. And the results are here for you to read.

JESSE LEE KERCHEVAL
Montevideo, Uruguay

MIGUEL AVERO

translation by Jona Colson

Sea Breaking Open

The night disintegrates
over the brightness of the umbrellas,
over the countless skins
gradually hardened.
In the folds of the quivering breeze
air and water are the same.
Individuals rush
trampling the perplexed mirrors
of the street.
A gray smoke
has supplanted the nocturnal light.
A man's grin
at each corner
gathered
under a sky
shattered so many times.
The child and his smile
behind a blue window
like the dream of fish
and above the earth
a sea breaking open.

Mar descascarado

Se desintegra la noche
sobre el resplandor de los paraguas,
sobre las innumerables pieles
poco a poco endurecidas.
En los pliegues de la estremecida brisa
aire y agua son lo mismo.
Individuos apurados
pisoteando los espejos
perplejos de la calle.
Nocturna luz
que un humo gris ha suplantado.
La mueca del hombre
en cada esquina
reunida
ante un cielo
desmoronado tantas veces.
El niño y su sonrisa
tras una ventana azul
como el sueño de los peces
y encima de la tierra
un mar descascarado.

Waters

Water in the tar-dark morning

or at night where the cardboard boxes
block the sunrise.

Water nesting on rooftops.

Water in the plaza
where the stars
forgot their black holes.

Constant water,
occasional water.

Water in the reflection
that discovers
the eye in the mirror.

Water in the ink of the verses
that will never be written.

Water overflowing
the cold glass and drowned
with an immensurable drop.

Water in a troubled river
of our inner peace,
where we will never walk,
where no ashes remain.

Water settling
around the last fire.

Aguas

Agua en la mañana alquitranada

o en la noche que cubre
de cartones el amanecer.

Agua en los tejados anidando.

Agua en la explanada
donde olvidaron sus agujeros
negros las estrellas.

Agua incesante,
agua de a ratos.

Agua en el reflejo
que descubre
el ojo en el espejo.

Agua en la tinta de los versos
que no se escribirán nunca.

Agua rebasando
el vaso frío y ahogado
con una gota inestimable.

Agua en el revuelto río
de nuestra paz interior,
donde jamás caminaremos,
donde ni cenizas quedan.

Agua acampando
en torno al último fogón.

Argument

The image that we cast
into the darkness,
wet mist and ash
of a late evening,
now stirs
before us.

Everything that passes before our eyes
we call illusion.
The water that sweeps the steps,
the early night
darkening time,
its ink-stained hands harassing
the columns of the planet.

We will never know what happens
behind the blinds of others,
behind the pupils
where a single image
slides
its truth lying to us all.

The pieces of this puzzle
one by one become detached,

relentlessly

different.

In every man the rain
weaves its argument.

Argumento

La imagen que echamos
al olvido,
bruma húmeda y ceniza
de cierta tarde envejecida,
se agita ahora
ante nosotros.

Todo cuanto pase ante los ojos
llamemos ilusión.
El agua que barre los peldaños,
la prematura noche
oscureciendo el tiempo,
sus manos tintas acosando
las columnas del planeta.

Nunca sabremos lo que ocurre
detrás de las persianas de los otros,
detrás de las pupilas
donde una imagen
remota se desliza
mintiéndonos a todos su verdad.

Las piezas de este puzzle
una a una se desprenden,

sin tregua,

distintas.

En cada hombre la lluvia
teje su argumento.

Like a Sheet

the ocean retreated,
all resurfaced with its most violent face,
with its face of nothing,
with its stillness of death.

Lives that turned to stone
from love of the depths,
mystery unveiled,
crystal of false clarity.

Mountains that were made small,
houses that shine, fish in the windows,
and from now the impossibility

of valuing a coin,
of marking the rainbow,
of trusting agreements.

Como una lámina

se retiró el océano,
todo resurgió con su rostro más violento,
con su cara de nada,
con su quietud de muerte.

Vidas que se volvieron piedra
de amar las profundidades,
misterio develado,
cristal de falsa diafanidad.

Montañas que se hicieron pequeñas,
casas que lucieron peces en sus ventanas
y desde ahora la imposibilidad

de valorar una moneda,
de señalar el arco iris,
o de confiar en pactos.

That Sea

That deep sea between us
or distance that unites us
without hope,

still and low air
like a street where the words crossed.
A corner we will someday have to face;

to account for the last embraces
when they are extinguished,

the last gray ashes of the kisses,
the last sounds
of a fine rain that was
cloak and happiness.

Even though
we called that weather intemperate
and the gentle breeze
silence.

Ese mar

Ese mar profundo entre nosotros
o distancia que nos une
sin remedio,

aire quieto y bajo
como una calle donde cruzaron las palabras.
Esquina que algún día tendremos que enfrentar;

rendir cuentas de los últimos abrazos
cuando estos se hayan extinguido,

las últimas cenizas grises de los besos,
los últimos sonidos
de un fino llover que era
capa y felicidad.

Por más
que a aquel tiempo le llamamos intemperie
y a la suave brisa aquella
le decíamos silencio.

MARTÍN BAREA MATTOS
translation by Mark Statman

from *By Hour, by Day, by Month*

In the water's depth
where the motors stop
I sleep

and I die without dying
and I dream that I die
and in reality
I sleep

and they say it's like that
in death
life
only a dream

and I find the secret

of the submerged clock
and my diluted mirror
and now I can't remember
now can't remember its purpose

and I prefer tonight
to remain awake
with open eyes
in the water's depth

by the light of the moon
or should I say the zenith of the river
in the profound depth of the sun

that goes that way
awake
dying and dreaming and returns
dying to dream

each new day
again
new
each day

new again

new.

From my brow falls a drop
on the lake of my name
from my name a drop falls
on the lake of my brow

without care
without memory or forgetting
with precision
the cared-for body
that working I extinguish

and my leather soul loses and rests

by
a drop
giving
vision
of
water.

On my house's corner there's a great wasteland
between the church and my house
great wasteland of great success

    small failure
           devastating the land
                                    of a great work

the ocean is a wasteland where the television arrived
pawning my grandmother's jewels
familiar plunder of control
remote battalion
the tomb
this clandestine wasteland of homeland
of the jingle hymn and song
or a profaned house
of alarms without landlord.

They put before the machines
before other eyes
already pneumatic

and there are the neighbors
the dogs cats birds

singing rodents and pedestrians level with the earth

and each one smokes
their carbon dioxide
their tar and nicotine words
crossing kisses

and they shake hands with branches streets corners
like you
like voices forever.

This drink of water that is curved and rambling and walled and
    drools among the rocks

this glass of water that is table and dream and serpent and sheet
that is river mineral ocean and slave
that is my water my body my bed
this lip that is rain and words and umbrellas
and salivated tiles and wet stockings
and laundry and rope and asphalt roof
and beach and hook and bucket and sand and mermaid beached
and a castle without centuries
and shore with children
and chinese equal drops
and tortures and turns of the century
and great the wave and destiny
and the suicide and the nothing swimming
and the foam and the soap and the shower and vapor
ends with the spiral shell guarding
the sound deeply read.

Code

Honor
I give you my word
I give you my poem
I return the silence
and the possibility
of being betrayed
you give me your word
another
poem
and silence
I have no option
I give my word.

Terror is theft
a dying at the hands of another

terrorism repeats the stolen and the stealing
and teaches stealing
the culture of stealing
the terror rises
and teaches terror
the theft of death
the culture teaches
Now . . . repeat

From the new map
I couldn't
Not even helped by astronomy
show you the sky of zeros and ones
the lost point of the ball of thread
in the virtual buttonhole
of history.

Adopted or adapted
the same
so no one finds out who is your mother or father
there is a system that registers difference
don't be afraid between family and infamy
the circle of chairs
the time to betray
between prayer and portion there is a father
your old age will be the same
if you remember the difference

the same.

Because all the dead
still innocent
still make fun of life

hairless skull
your smile
is mine.

de *Por hora, por día, por mes*

En el fondo del agua
dónde los motores
se apagan
me duermo

y muero sin morir
y sueño que muero
y en la realidad
duermo

y dicen qué tal es
en muerte
la vida
solo un sueño

y encuentro

el secreto del reloj sumergido
y mi espejo diluido
y ya no recuerdo ya no recuerdo su objeto

y prefiero esta noche
quedarme despierto con los ojos abiertos
en el fondo del agua

a la luz de la luna o debo decir
en el cenit del río
en el fondo profundo del sol

qué anda por ahí despierto

muriendo y soñando
y vuelve

muriendo a soñar
cada día

nuevo de nuevo.

Mi frente deja caer una gota
sobre la laguna de mi nombre
mi nombre deja caer una gota
sobre la laguna de mi frente

sin cuidado recuerdo y olvido
a rigor el cuerpo cuidador
que extingo trabajando

y mi alma de cuero pierde y descansa

a gota
da
mirada
de
agua.

En la esquina de mi casa un gran baldío
entre la iglesia y mi casa
el gran baldío del gran éxito

fracaso pequeño
      asolando el solar
                                     de la gran obra

el océano es el baldío por donde llegó televisión empeñando
las joyas de mi abuela
saqueos familiares a control

**remoto batallón
la tumba
ese baldío clandestino de la patria
del yingle himno y canción
o una casa profanada
de alarma sin patrón.**

Los ponen ante máquinas
ante otros ojos
ya neumáticos

y ahí son vecinos
los perros los gatos los pájaros

cantando roedores y peatones a ras de la tierra

y cada uno fuma
su anhídrido carbónico
sus palabras nicotina y alquitrán asfálticas
recorriendo besos
y apretón de ramas de calles de esquinas
como vos
como voces para siempre.

Este trago de agua que es curva y rambla y muro y baba entre las
    rocas
este vaso con agua que es mesa y sueño y serpiente y sábana
que es río mineral océano y esclava
que es mi agua mi cuerpo y mi cama
este labio que es lluvia y palabra y paraguas
y baldosa salivada y medias mojadas
y lavarropas
y cuerda y azotea asfaltada
y playa y anzuelo y balde y arena y sirena encallada

y castillo sin siglos
y orilla con niños
y gotas iguales como chinos
y torturas y cambio de siglo
y grande la ola y el destino
y el suicidio y la nada a nado
y la espuma y el jabón y la ducha y el vapor
termina en caracol guardando
el sonido leído.

Código

Honor
te doy mi palabra
te doy mi poema
te devuelvo el silencio
y la posibilidad
de ser traicionado
me das tu palabra
otro
poema
y el silencio
y no tengo opción
te doy mi palabra.

El terror es plagio
como morir a manos de otro
terrorismo repetir lo plagiado y plagiar
y enseñar a plagiar
la cultura del plagio
y al terror izar
y enseñar el terror
lo plagiado la muerte
la cultura a enseñar
repetid. . .

**Del nuevo mapa
no podría
ni ayudado por la astronomía**

enseñarte el cielo de ceros y unos

**la punta perdida del ovillo
en el ojal virtual
de la historia.**

Adoptado o adaptado
da igual
que nadie se entere quién es tu padre o madre
hay un sistema que registra la diferencia
no te asustes entre la familia y la infamia
el círculo de sillas
el turno de fregar
entre la oración y la ración hay un padre
tu vejez será igual
si recuerdas la diferencia

será igual.

**Porque todos los muertos
inocentes todavía
construyen la mueca todavía de la vida**

**pelada calavera
tu sonrisa
es la mía.**

HORACIO CAVALLO AND FRANCISCO TOMSICH

translation by Geoffrey Brock

Hermes

I.
Crickets are errors in the silence, or so
thinks sleepless Hermes, in his boxer shorts.
Chin on his fist, packet of cigarettes
beneath the portrait of Florencio.

The moon, the window: up and down his street
populations of neighbors and of crickets.
The night is hung from clothespins like a blanket
and Hermes dreams of a long, silent retreat.

He flops back on the bed, lets one hand stray
across the mattress toward the empty half,
hoping for company (pleasure held at bay)

that never comes. He spends his night like this:
hearing the chirps, smoking, and putting off
the mythic founding of his moodiness.

Hermes

I.
Los grillos son errores del silencio
se dice Hermes insomne, en calzoncillos.
El puño en el mentón, los cigarrillos
debajo del cuadrito de Florencio.

La luna, la ventana: calle Ascencio,
poblada de vecinos y de grillos;
la noche está colgada con palillos
y él sueña con gestores del silencio.

Se tira así vestido, tienta el lado
vacío de la cama de dos plazas,
y espera, conteniendo la garufa

visitas impensables. Trasnochado,
oyendo el cricriquear, fuma y aplaza
la Fundación Tercera de la mufa.

Hermes

V.
The cricket's saying terrifying things
to the boy regarding it with a kind stare,
who quickly but not without a certain care
places it in a little jar with rings

of air holes in the lid. Hermes looks on,
thinking about Toquinho's "Testament,"
the tune the insect strums in the event
its jar is shaken. Later he puts his own

repository in their little pasture,
meaning to gather cricket after cricket
into a tiny funerary pyre.

The boy, appalled, can't bear to look at it;
he hurtles from the scene like an aria
as Hermes nervously rolls a cigarette.

Hermes

V.
El grillo dice cosas pavorosas
al niño que lo mira con cariño
y sin vacilación ni desaliño,
lo mete en un frasquito de curiosas

ranuras. Hermes mira, piensa cosas
sobre ese "Testamento" de Toquinho
que improvisa el insecto cuando el niño
agita y bate el frasco; luego posa

su propio recipiente en el pastito;
propone unir allí grillo con grillo
en una mini pira funeraria.

El niño horrorizado mira ahíto
y sale disparado como un aria
cuando Hermes arma ansioso un cigarrillo.

Icarus

III.
Poor Daedalus advised his only son:
follow me, child, but keep to the middle sky,
for the sun ruins things that go too high.
Your path, my dear, must be a level one . . .

But Icarus, tired of warnings, hasn't heard.
He launches into the air to test his wings,
and from on high, where heat does ruin things,
an object can be seen to fall, a blurred

bundle of cords and feathers. A boatman,
smoking a cigarette on deck, looks up
as absentmindedly he fills his cup

and says to his invisible companion:
I made a wish, old pal, seeing as I
just saw a shooting star fall from the sky.

Ícaro

III.
Dédalo, desgraciado, dijo al hijo:
seguí por donde voy, no tan arriba,
que allá el calor del sol todo derriba,
mantén querido mío un punto fijo.

Pero Ícaro no escucha ese prolijo
concepto y se lanza a la deriva.
De allá donde el calor todo derriba
se ha visto caer algo, un amasijo

de plumas y tendones. Un barquero
que fuma un cigarrillo en plena popa
mirando sin mirar llena una copa

y dice al invisible compañero:
pedí un deseo, hermano, que estoy viendo
una estrella fugaz que va cayendo.

Icarus

V.
As soon as he hits the water's icy surface
he looks around, expecting a lifeboat.
But water's all he sees. Time's running out:
the sun is going down. Poor Icarus

then understands and smiles, but wearily.
With a beneficent revenge in mind,
he launches himself at once across the sea,
and when the day star sinks into the stunned

horizon, he fills again with a sudden joy—
in the sea's mirror he finds what he's been seeking:
the blood-drenched sun, and at its heart a boy.

Now he feels sad again, and he can't think.
The boat has not yet come for him, and something
is tugging him down. Now he starts to sink.

Ícaro

V.
Apenas en el agua resfriado,
Ícaro espera balsa salvadora.
Ya solo el agua pasa; se hace hora:
el sol se viene abajo. El desgraciado

comprende y se sonríe adormilado.
Pensando una venganza bienhechora
se lanza mar arriba sin demora
y cuando el astro se hunde en el helado

horizonte se renueva de alegría;
en el reflejo está lo que quería:
el sol ensangrentado, y él su centro.

Entonces entristece, se confunde.
La balsa no aparece, y algo dentro
del mar lo tironea. Ya se hunde.

Games

V.
The house feels empty. Faucets can be heard
doing poor impressions of a second hand.
One windowpane is broken, and the wind
hangs plaintive whistles on a standing shard.

Two men regard each other. One feels hope.
The other's brooding over an old saddle:
lost in thought, his thumb and finger fiddle
with leather straps. He's mulling his escape,

how he might disappear without a trace
then reappear again in some far-off place
with death clinging quietly to his chest.

But none will see him on the roadway, since
the pull of evening is stronger, of indolence
and willow shadows, and of the need to rest.

Juegos

V.
La casa está vacía. La gotera
imita un impreciso segundero.
El viento cuelga un silbo lastimero
del rastro del cristal en la madera.

Los dos hombres se miran. Uno espera.
El otro le da vueltas al apero;
ensimismado juega con el cuero
rumiando la evasión, una manera

de desaparecer sin dejar rastro
y aparecerse así a campo traviesa
con una silenciosa muerte a cuestas.

Pero no lo verán sobre el balastro:
más fuertes son la tarde y la pereza,
las sombras de los sauces y las siestas.

MARTÍN CERISOLA
translation by Keith Ekiss

from *Something Naked*

> All the beautiful phrases spoken about transcending nature prove ineffectual in the face of the primordial forces of life.
>
> —FRANK KAFKA, *Diaries*

A cemetery of elephants.   26
A vast territory of immense white bones.

Suddenly, in a corner, the gentle movements
of a baby elephant. The innocent trembling of its
trunk, its swinging feet; a look, cheerful
among the bones.

Fragile bud among the rigid forms.

New-born word.

His eyes were wild.   27
The movements of his body seemed broken, without
continuity, panting. Also, the grimaces of his
face, like tics in the eyes and mouth; fingers
stiff as dissected insects.
With one hand he squeezed his bulge and shook it
inside his pants.
He looked at us each in turn, giving us
a stare, soaked with greed and alcohol.

None of us wanted to be that man.

Enter into life. Like spending a force   31
that won't stop struggling.
Without any film. Completely naked.

To gain access.
Without evading the space all around. Without scenarios in mind. (Always the same voices saying the
same things.)

Step aside.
Purify.
Exit.

Continue without a self.

Long ago (or as children) the body crossed
the day with the force put there. Graceful.
Consciousness and the energy that consumed
the consciousness that followed.
At first it was the body. The fight, the delivery,
throughout the day and throughout the night.

We lost the adventure, became civilized.
We cannot stray more than over geometric
roads others have laid out. We long
for rituals like exorcisms; we are that scream
in the painting that puts fear on our faces
resigned to what is coming.

Life calls us to undo. But we inhabit the fear.

Resign ourselves to this and that. We spawn, incomplete buds. We see, in others, life, and we applaud.

And we clench our teeth.
Every night.

Each suicide is as if we are not born.

Something was speaking in that minimal light.   35
It was silent and trembling on the wall as an
animal with cold.
Something opened that minute, and it stopped me
its imperceptible movement.

Its seed.

de *Algo se desnuda*

> Todas las bellas palabras que hablan de trascender la naturaleza se demuestran ineficaces frente a los poderes primordiales de la vida.
> —FRANZ KAFKA, *Diarios*

Un cementerio de elefantes.
Un vasto territorio de huesos blancos, inmensos.

De pronto, en un rincón, los movimientos mansos
de un elefante niño. El temblor inocente de su
trompa, sus patas oscilantes; la mirada, alegre
entre los huesos.

Frágil brote entre la rigidez de las formas.

Palabra naciente.

Tenía los ojos desencajados.
Los movimientos del cuerpo parecían rotos, sin
continuidad, jadeantes. También los gestos de la
cara, como tics en la mirada y en la boca; los dedos
tiesos como insectos disecados.
Con una mano se apretaba el bulto y lo sacudía
por adentro del pantalón.
Nos miraba a todos, daba vueltas y nos recorría
con la mirada, húmeda de avidez y alcohol.

Todos queríamos no ser ese hombre.

Ir entrando en la vida. Como gastando una fuerza
que no acaba de pujar.
Sin ninguna película. Todo desnudez.

Acceder.
Sin evadir el espacio, alrededor. Sin escenarios de la mente. (Son siempre las mismas voces diciendo las mismas cosas.)

Apartarse.
Afinar.
Salir.

Seguir sin uno mismo.

Antiguamente (o de niños) el cuerpo atravesaba 32
el día con la fuerza puesta allí. Desenvuelta.
La conciencia, y la energía que consume la conciencia,
vino después.
Al principio era el cuerpo. La lucha, la entrega, a
lo largo del día y a lo largo de la noche.

Hemos perdido la aventura civilizándonos.
No podemos errar más que sobre caminos
geométricos que otros dispusieron. Anhelamos
rituales como exorcismos; somos ese grito en la
pintura que harán de nuestras caras de espanto
resignado los venideros.

La vida llama a deshacer. Pero habitamos el miedo.

Resignamos esto y aquello. Incubamos brotes truncos.
Vemos, en otros, la vida, y la aplaudimos.

Y apretamos los dientes.
Cada noche.

Cada suicidio de lo que no nacemos.

Algo estaba diciendo aquella mínima luz. 35
Era silencio y temblaba en la pared como un
animal con frío.
Algo abría ese minuto, y me detuvo
su imperceptible movimiento.

Su semilla.

Untitled

1.
It's there—in the fire.
In the radiant wound of light where newborns burn and what's pure is mixed and where the flames are never the same; they are the wind inside and what the wind devours, what is reduced to ashes. As the red of dawn, the fire consumed the bones of what would be born another way.

2.
A ghost.
An unheard voice.
Someone
like dancing in another world
visits me,
leaves me.
Its wake sinks further than what's possible.
Red.
Like the mark of a burn.

3.
Life is wide awake.
Life opens.
Each time.
Inviting.

And quietly, without anyone noticing, love happens.
Fulfilled. Nothing's more alive than the secret life.

4.
Dance to leave your sick fixation in the white.
To feel your hands empty and alive.
Because there is no brighter word than one as yet unknown.
One that gives life.

5.
Release beauty.
As if it were unbounded toward the throat's sea.
Metal. Song. Shoal.

That wound. It's a girl.

Don't let the scar surround you.

Don't look.

6.
To write.
To release, like a mouth of birds, the woods, with their noise of rain
and crowns shaken by the wind.

Sin título

1.
Es allí, desde el fuego.
Desde la incandescente herida de la luz donde arden los nacientes, y lo puro es mezcla, y las llamas son nunca las mismas, y son el viento en ellas y son también lo que devoran,
lo que reducen a ceniza.
Como lo rojo del alba, el fuego consume los huesos de lo que va a nacer de otra manera.

2.
Un fantasma.
Una voz que no se oye.
Alguien
como bailando en otro mundo
me visita,
me deja.
Su estela se hunde más allá de lo posible.
Roja.
Como la marca de una quemadura.

3.
La vida está despierta.
La vida se abre.
Cada vez.
Invita.

Y en silencio, sin que nadie lo advierta, el amor sucede.
Se cumple.
No hay nada más vivo que la vida secreta.

4.
Baila para salir de su enfermedad de fijeza en el blanco.
Para sentir las manos vacías y estar vivo.

Porque no hay palabra más encendida que la que todavía no sabe.
La que vivir le regala.

5.
Soltar la hermosura.
Como si fuera sin límites hacia el mar de la garganta.
Metal. Canción. Cardumen.

Esa herida. Es niña.

No dejes que la cicatriz la alcance.

No la mires.

6.
Escribir.
Soltar, como una boca de pájaros, el bosque, con su ruido de
 lluvia
y copas sacudidas por el viento.

LAURA CESARCO EGLIN

translation by Lauren Shapiro

Downpour

A gray sky's anxiety
knotted with the timbre of clouds
unloading itself in buckets to recycle the sea
to free itself from the urge to peel back
screams, to leave them naked
in hoarse thunderclaps and lightning
the sea keeps licking the sand
to shape it more than the wind
the steps that leave their prints
are erased, disappearing
like they disappeared you
leaving me with one less fingerprint
with each question that I refused to answer
while today the grayness swells
over the weeping, thundering its images
its electric shock after shock is
what remains of you.

Aguacero

La ansiedad de un cielo gris
apelotonado en tonos de nubes
descargándose a cántaros para reciclar el mar
para liberar las ganas de pelar
gritos, dejarlos desnudos
en truenos roncos y relámpagos
el mar sigue lamiendo la arena
para moldearla más que el viento
las pisadas que ahuellan
se borran desapareciendo
como te desaparecieron a vos
dejándome con una huella menos
con cada pregunta que me negué a contestar
mientras hoy el gris se hincha
de todo el llanto, relampaguean imágenes
que entre picana y picana es
lo que queda de vos.

Agency

I don't need a kaleidoscope when I can
lie down and close my eyes, my gaze fixed
on a window and my breathing arming the wavering
of the light, arming what I will not name, will not give
stillness, so that it happens in spite of me
although I know that when the mountain melts
and the cork branches out, I will be in Portugal; the wind
gusts to its side, leaves loosen themselves, some
underneath this pen also indicate the course
of the current today without needing to wet the tip
of the finger to feel where it comes from,
I don't see it coming; it's here, time's ventriloquist
says that I say that it says that I say
I say

Agencia

No necesito un caleidoscopio cuando puedo
acostarme con los ojos cerrados, la mirada dirigida
a una ventana y la respiración arma los vaivenes
de la luz, arma lo que no nombro para no darle
quietud, que siga pasando como a pesar de mí
aunque sé bien que cuando la montaña se derrita
y el corcho se ramifique estaré en Portugal; el viento
tironea para su lado, se desatan hojas, alguna que
otra bajo esta lapicera también indica cómo va
la corriente hoy sin necesidad de mojar la punta
del dedo para sentir de dónde viene
lo demás, no lo veo venir; está acá, ventrílocuo
del tiempo dice que yo digo que dice que digo
digo

If the Storm Can

    Renata stared because no other verb occurred to her to apply to the situation. At some point the yellow would stop being only egg yolk, and she would be there to orchestrate the change. The pitch of her name in each person set off a train she was conducting—some headed east, taking grayness with them like someone turning a page. She didn't know how the station would be afterward; she had never been convinced by stillness, and each time she decided not to look back.

Si la tormenta puede

Renata miraba porque no se le ocurría ningún otro verbo para aplicar a la situación. En algún momento el amarillo dejaría de ser sólo yema, y ella estaría ahí para percusionar el cambio. El tono de su nombre en cada persona comenzaba un tren y lo dirigía —algunos hacia el Este, llevándose el gris como quien cambia de hoja. No sabía cómo quedaba la estación después; eso de estar estático nunca la convenció y decidía cada vez no mirar atrás.

Pasta with Tomato Sauce

Federico Roca's vomit
photogram photogram photogram
plunging down the stairs
the frame of the stair cuts
from Federico to my memory in the photograph
the noodles rushing
plunging in bile
my memory moves against that current
the stairs of the school
erasing the evidence to clean the traces, Celeste came
to look for the vomit, her job demanded this
mine was to fight over the trash
that Celeste sweeps in a movie
    Federico Roca falling
as if he knew he had left
the noodles I saw
I remember Federico Roca's vomit plunging
down the stairs of the school.

Tuco con una buena pasta

El vómito de Federico Roca
fotograma fotograma fotograma
cayéndose por las escaleras
el marco del escalón hace los cortes
desde Federico a mi memoria en fotografía
los fideos yéndose
cayendo en bilis
mi recuerdo va en contra de esa corriente
las escaleras de la escuela
borrar evidencias para limpiar rastros, Celeste vino
a buscar el vómito, su trabajo la obligaba a eso
el mío a disputar la basura
que Celeste barre en una película
     Federico Roca cayéndose
miraba sabiendo que él se había ido
los fideos que vi
Recuerdo el vómito de Federico Roca cayéndose
por las escaleras de la escuela.

Photogenic

I.
She turns around and doesn't look at the camera. She looks at us. She leaves the frame. She brings us, little by little, one by one, together. The photo, without her. She takes from us what comes from others. Those features that reveal the ones she lost in the war. To take a photo is to resist remembrance. To look at a photo while it's being taken is to help her recover the memory.

II.
She would find herself in the photo. In the one of her family that she wanted to show me. To show me in order to recognize herself. If she doesn't come through in this photo maybe she'll return with those who aren't here. If she looks at us, maybe she'll see them. If again she finds that place on the border of the frame, they will also see us. That place in the eye, with which one sees what is faint, is precisely between the two photos. She knows that she has to see if it can be done; to disrupt the development, to return the third person plural to the intimacy of the first person, plural, singular.

III.
When I look at the photo we are there, as is her shaved head. A flash in the eyes is a flashback in her history. It hurts. Persists. She attaches herself to abandonment—to being the only survivor in the family. She looks at us in order to be kept company. She doesn't look to overcome the forever of afterward. If she would look at the camera, it would capture the fractions of her that remain.

Fotogénica

I.
Se da vuelta y no mira a la cámara. Nos mira a nosotros. Sale del marco. Nos toma ella, de a poco, uno a uno, todos juntos. Sin ella, la foto. Toma de nosotros lo que viene de otros. Esos rasgos que revelan a los que perdió con la guerra. Sacar una foto es contrarrestar la memoria. Mirar la foto mientras es sacada es ayudarla a recuperar el recuerdo.

II.
Se encontraría en la foto. En esa de su familia que le gustaría mostrarme. Mostrarme para reconocerse. Si no sale en esta foto tal vez vuelva con los que no están. Si nos mira, tal vez los pueda ver en nosotros. Si encuentra otra vez ese lugar en el borde del marco, ellos nos podrán ver también. Ese lugar del ojo, con el que uno ve lo tenue, está justamente ahí, entre las dos fotos. Sabe que hay que ver si se puede; desordenar el revelado, volver la tercera persona del plural a la intimidad de la primera persona, plural, singular.

III.
Cuando miro la foto estamos, como están sus cabellos, cortados. Un flash a los ojos es un flashback en su historia. Duele. Persiste. Se apega al desamparo–ser la única sobreviviente de la familia. Nos mira para estar acompañada. No mira para obviar el para siempre del después. Si mirara a la cámara, ésta captaría las fracciones de la que está.

LAURA CHALAR

translation by Erica Mena

avenida 18 de julio

if walt whitman were here, how he would sing of them and sing to them with the deep voice of a street prophet, dedicating the hymn of his long grey vigil to the dark flock of the gentle poor, ant citizens, his hand touching the woman who waits at the bus stop, the policeman, the scavenger, the law clerk in his exhausted shoes, the begging children, the begging elderly, the fat salesgirls, the kids spilling out of the law school, the *garrapiñero*, the watchband seller, the half-blind lottery ticket seller, the supreme court judge who is running late again, the man who just bought a smartphone, the woman who recites poems on the bus, the shoe shiner, the people handing out flyers for loan sharks or massage parlors, and me, who watches it all with the love of someone who is bound to leave, someone who is already leaving.

por dieciocho

si estuviera walt whitman acá, cómo los cantaría y les cantaría con su ronca voz de augur callejero, dedicándole su himno de larga vigilia gris a la oscura grey de pobres mansos, ciudadanía de hormigas, tocando con su mano a la que espera en la parada, al policía, al hurgador, al procurador cansado en sus zapatos, a los niños que piden, a los viejos que piden, a las gordas de la expo, a los chiquilines que salen de facultad, al garrapiñero, al del puestito de correas de reloj, al quinielero medio ciego, al ministro de la suprema corte que una vez más llega tarde, al que se compró el celular con internet, a la que recita poemas en el ómnibus, al lustrabotas, a las que reparten volantes de usureros o casas de masajes y a mí, que miro todo con el amor de quien se va, quien se está yendo.

Montevideo

I.
The sea light rises
over sleeping streets,
and the wind tangles violet clouds
in the great amphitheater of the night.

II.
Cordón

With gray fingers the rain
comes sketching the trees.
Behind the closed windows
people wake to Sunday.
And the broken floor tiles shine
like the poor in their best dress.

III.
Rambla

Sand and granite curve
beneath a long mirage.
Further out, the tongue
of the breakwater stretches.

IV.
The jacaranda afternoon
stretched over the boat-shaped house.
The air swirled with shards of sun
and sparrows in noisy filigree.

V.
Port

Summer crackled down the street
toward the sea. A slow potbellied freighter
cut the hard glare of the surge,
uprooting splinters of light like signals
from the incandescent arc of the bay.

Montevideo

I.
Sube luz de mar
por las calles dormidas,
y el viento enreda nubes violetas
en el alto anfiteatro de la noche.

II.
Cordón

Con dedos grises la lluvia
va dibujando los árboles.
Tras las calladas ventanas
nace la gente al domingo.
Y brillan las baldosas rotas
como pobres en sus galas.

III.
Rambla

Arena y granito ondulan
bajo un largo espejismo.
Más lejos, se despereza
la lengua de la escollera.

IV.
La tarde del jacarandá
se tendió sobre la casa-barco.
En el aire giraban esquirlas de sol
y gorriones en inquieta filigrana.

V.
Puerto

Crepitaba el verano calle abajo,
camino al mar. Un carguero panzudo y despacioso
cortaba el brillo duro de las aguas,
arrancando astillas de luz como señales
al arco incandescente de la bahía.

Helsinki

When that bitter rag gets rammed in her throat, which may happen several times during a standard day, she closes her eyes and imagines herself in Helsinki.

The air draws blood from those who breathe it, the sun smoothes the streets, the architecture of the city bares its long grin of windows to passersby. People have hair like snow and eyes like water. Their skin is transparent, I mean, you could even say there is no skin; but that clarity is common in cold climates. It's difficult to lie with such an exposed face. And so, when someone says to someone, "Minä rakastan sinua," that someone (the latter) immediately knows if it is true.

When all faces around her are closed, when voices are covered in ash, she closes her eyes and is in Helsinki. Under the protection of Jean Sibelius and of General Mannerheim and of students playing hooky in Esplanade Park. The style of the buildings is called "neo-Renaissance," but we'll try to say it in poems.

When the hours asphyxiate her, she closes her eyes and is in Helsinki. Predictably, it's cold. She should have put on a jacket.

Helsinki

Cuando ese trapo amaro se le atasca en la garganta, lo cual puede llegar a ocurrir varias veces a lo largo de un día standard, cierra los ojos y se imagina que está en Helsinki.

El aire puede hacer sangrar a quien respira, el sol pule las avenidas, la arquitectura de la ciudad muestra a los transeúntes su larga sonrisa de ventanas. La gente tiene pelo como nieve y ojos como agua. La piel es transparente, es decir, podría decirse que no hay piel; pero esta pureza es común en los climas fríos. Es difícil mentir a cara descubierta. Por eso, cuando alguien le dice a alguien "Minä rakastan sinua", ese alguien (el segundo) enseguida sabe si es verdad.

Cuando las miradas a su alrededor se cierren, cuando las voces se cubren de ceniza, cierra los ojos y está en Helsinki. Bajo la protección de Jean Sibelius y del general Mannerheim y de los estudiantes rateados del colegio que pasean por el Parque de la Explanada. El estilo de los edificios se llama neorrenacentista, pero trataremos de decirlo en poemas.

Cuando las horas asfixian, cierra los ojos y está en Helsinki. Previsiblemente, hace frío. Tendría que haberse puesto una campera.

Guest

> Are not five sparrows sold for two farthings,
> and not one of them is forgotten before God?
>
> —LUKE 12:6

The heart of the bird became the heart of the home. It pulsed from the kitchen like a red seed, though it was nothing more than the heart of a bird, kept in its cage of feathers and little bones.

And the heart was to the bird as the bird was to the house. It awaited its hour filling the space of itself, just like the first letter of an illuminated manuscript. It was not a motionless waiting, because the heart also chirped, and practiced fluttering its wings, a prelude to the great flight of someday.

Sometimes it kept watch, the bird, and sometimes it slept. And when it slept we knew that the night would be more alive, large with poplars and the fast sky of the dreams it dreamed, and then we didn't go into the kitchen: we went to bed without the glass of water, content with the heart of the bird in the house.

There was golden air, high blue air, and no walls in the dreams that the bird dreamed. That's why it died.

But I want to be where you are, little broken light.

Huésped

¿No se venden cinco pajarillos por dos moneditas?
Sin embargo, Dios no se olvida de ninguno de ellos.

—LUCAS 12:6

El corazón del pájaro se volvió el corazón de la casa. Latía desde la cocina como una semilla roja, aunque no fuera más que un corazón del pájaro, guardado en su caja de pluma y huesitos.

Y el corazón era el pájaro como el pájaro a la casa. Aguardaba su hora llenando el espacio de sí mismo, al igual que una inicial iluminada en un manuscrito. No era una espera inmóvil, porque el corazón también piaba, ensayaba estrépitos de alas, preludio del gran vuelo de algún día.

A veces velaba, el pájaro, y a veces dormía. Y cuando dormía sabíamos que la noche sería más viva, grande de álamo y cielo veloz de los sueños que él soñaba, y entonces no entrábamos a la cocina: nos íbamos a acostar sin el vaso de agua, contentos del corazón del pájaro en la casa.

Había aire dorado, alto aire azul y sin muros en los sueños que soñaba el pájaro. Por eso se murió.

Pero yo quiero estar donde tú estás, pequeña luz quebrada.

Poligrillo

a ringdove chick
Flurry of ugly feathers
and bald angles
thin beak and warm legs
shipwrecked
tiny vagrant
promenade of *peep* people
in the kitchen

domestic flights
floor to counter

you little dove,
Poligrillo.

Poligrillo

un pichón de torcaza
Revuelo de plumas feas
y rincones pelados
náufrago
pico flaco y patas tibias
pequeño bichicome
promenade de gente *pip*
en la cocina

vuelos de cabotaje
suelo/mesada

palomita.
Poligrillo.

ANDREA DURLACHER

translation by Anna Rosenwong

Untitled

I'm not like other ladies:
the street soaks up my wanting
to free myself from grief
(the street,
the very street
otherworldly object
that doesn't double back
the street like a broken object that attacks the feeling of
    [faces
shortly before they're paralyzed
or go on the defensive)

Once I was happy and I didn't think about all that.

I fear the street
and the lady still speaking to another lady
and I think of myself

and I see the faces, how they suffer like the street.

And the lady innocently toys with the little spoon.
She holds a cup of coffee
and does not worry.

Sin título

No soy como otras damas:
la calle me absorbe las ganas
de librarme de la angustia
(la calle,
justo la calle,
otro objeto del mundo
que no se retuerce
la calle como un objeto roto que ataca la sensibilidad de los
 [rostros
poco antes de que se paralicen
o se coloque a la defensiva)

Antes era feliz y no pensaba en eso.

Le temo a la calle
y la dama habla todavía con la otra
y yo pienso en mí

y veo los rostros, que sufren como la calle.

Y la dama mueve con inocencia la cucharita.
Tiene el café enfrente
y no le preocupa.

Life Is as Much the Same as It Is Profane

We will flee between the rocks
we are disquisition.
The absolute outburst of destiny
go talk to someone else about free will, about human
 individuality!
What for?
Day after day we deny the hand of God that reaches down with
 [its bouquet of flowers
and knows before they're born just who the flowers are for.

God: you didn't grant me the gift of divining who the flowers are
 for
but you brought hundreds in your hand.
You carry them so happily they seem like garlands
and all I can do today is gaze at you covetously.

Sometimes I tell myself: between puddles we will walk hand in
 hand
like two children pretending to be pigs
we will entangle ourselves in a dirty game.

I need to see how you define the stream of your thought
how you sharpen the pain of your old age with the mere fact that
 [it is yours.
I may need . . . to run hand in hand with your very architecture.
I know who you are before even smelling your flowers.

You come to me as forward as you are divine
and I don't resist.
I let myself be carried away by your mouth
I smell your bouquet of flowers and become convinced I'll find
 [in them

your awesome idea for fixing the world.

La vida es tan mimísima como profana

Huiremos entre las rocas
somos la disquisición.
El arrebato absoluto del destino
¡y háblenle a otro del libre albedrío, de la individualidad
 humana!
¿Para qué?
Negamos día a día la mano de Dios que llega con su ramillete de
 [flores
y sabe antes de que las flores nazcan para quien serán.

Dios: no me diste la virtud de adivinar para quien serán las
 flores
pero traés cientos en tu mano.
Las llevas con tal alegría que me parecen guirnaldas
y hoy sólo me resta verte de reojo con cierta envidia.

A veces me digo: entre charcos andaremos de la mano
como dos niños que juegan a ser cerdos
nos enroscaremos en un juego sucio.

Yo preciso ver como definís tu vertiente
como intensificás los dolores de tu vejez por el mero hecho de
 [que es tuya.
Yo precisaría. . . correr de la mano con tu propia arquitectura.
Yo sé quien sos antes de siquiera oler tus flores.

Llegas a mí tan audaz como divino
no me niego.
Me dejo llevar por tu boca
huelo tu ramillete de flores y me convenzo de que se encuentra
 [allí

tu fabulosa idea para resolver el mundo.

Untitled

I begged the clock
not to count the hours
to wait for me a little
and not expect anything in return.

Under pressure
I don't want one hour to follow another.
And if they do
please don't carry me with the river
in the depths are fish I do not know.

Tic toc tic toc tiiiiiiiiiiiiiiic
I write each moment into long lines
when really it is short short, so short.
It's better that I write it down
to stop time from sinning.

My grandmother says the key is not to stay inside time
but outside my window the stoplight keeps changing colors all
    the time
and still

grows bored.

Hours aren't a question but an answer.
Even though time answers I put some faith in it
if I knew who to thank for my hopes
I might understand the meaning of faith.

Time passes in different colors for everyone
and they call me for dinnertime.

Sin título

Yo le rogaba al reloj
que no marcara las horas
que me esperara un poquito
y no me cobrara el favor.

Bajo presión
no quiero que una hora suceda a la otra.
Si le sucede
por favor no me lleve con el río
a lo hondo tiene peces que no conozco.

Tic tac tic tac tiiiiiiiiiiiiiiic
escribo de cada instante líneas largas
cuando en la verdad es corto corto, muy corto.
Mejor lo escribo,
para que la hora no peque.

Mi abuela dice que la clave es no quedarse en el tiempo
pero por la ventana el semáforo cambia de colores todo el
   tiempo
y aun así

se aburre.

Las horas no son una pregunta sino una respuesta.
Aunque el tiempo responda deposito en él alguna esperanza
si supiera a quien agradecer mis esperanzas
entendería el significado de la fe.

El tiempo pasa para todos en colores distintos
y me llaman a la hora de la cena.

Untitled

I left a trail like Hansel and Gretel's
and Hansel came back without Gretel
and Gretel peed in the grass.
Good weather brings bad harvests.
The world has a child's face.
Children are not do-gooders.
They're not like Lassie.

Lassie is a do-gooder dog.
I'm not.
I'm not a do-gooder.

I'm also not like Lassie because people don't want to
 [take care of me
or thank me for my courage.

I'm not a heroine
Lassie is.
Lassie is a do-gooder dog.

Lassie has her dog fan base.
Heaps of person friends.
Lassie is not a controversial dog.

I think: Lassie, Pluto, Goofy, Lady and the Tramp.
I haven't met a wide range of dogs.

Understand that Lassie
isn't like Pluto
isn't like Goofy.

A mission for Lassie:
round up Hansel and Gretel
and talk to the sun about drying that pee of Gretel's in the grass.

It can't be that tough.
Not for a dog like Lassie.
Lassie isn't like Pluto.
She's not like Goofy.
She's not like Lady or like the Tramp.
She's not a controversial dog.

She'll leap valleys and mountains
out of love for Hansel
or love for Gretel.

My bad weather will bring good harvests when Lassie comes
with the obedient idea of finding the sun
that'll dry Gretel's pee in the grass.

In the end, not all dogs are do-gooders.

Sometimes I come up with great ideas for fixing my life
    [in a flash
and right away they fall
like a herd of fatted calves.

(I was always one of those women
who even while putting a calf in the oven
turn politely to greet you)

It pains me to think about the real void inside things
meat without the word *meat*
or the calf
without its weak and trembling body.

In the evening I lie down in bed.
I want to sleep.
I can't.
Someone's voice echoes in my mind
and that is not meat.

Sin título

Hice como el camino de Hansel y Gretel
y Hansel volvió sin Gretel
y Gretel hizo pis en el pasto.
El buen tiempo trae malas cosechas.
El mundo tiene cara de nene.
Los nenes no son benefactores.
No son como Lassie.

Lassie es un perro benefactor.
Yo no.
No soy benefactora.

Tampoco soy como Lassie porque las personas no quieren
    [cuidarme
ni agradecen mi valentía.

No soy una heroína
y Lassie sí.
Lassie es un perro benefactor.

Lassie tiene su barra de fans perros.
Montones de amigas personas.
Lassie no es un perro polémico.

Pienso: Lassie, Pluto, Tribilín, la Dama y el Vagabundo.
No conocí a una amplia gama de perros.

Entiendan a Lassie
no es como Pluto
no es como Tribilín.

Misión para Lassie:
juntar a Hansel y a Gretel
y hablar con el sol para que seque el pis de Gretel en el pasto.

No puede ser tan difícil.
No para un perro como Lassie.
Lassie no es como Pluto.
No es como Tribilín.
No es como la Dama ni como el Vagabundo.
No es un perro polémico.

Saltaría valles y montañas
por amor a Hansel
o por amor a Gretel.

Mi mal tiempo traerá buenas cosechas cuando llegué Lassie
con la idea sumisa de encontrar al sol
que secara el pis de Gretel en el pasto.

Al final, no todos los perros son benefactores.

A menudo se me ocurren buenas ideas para resolver mi vida
 [en un momento
y enseguida caen
como una manada de terneros hartos.

(siempre fui de esas mujeres
que aun metiendo un ternero en el horno
gentilmente me voleaba a saludarte)

Me cuesta pensar en el vacío real de las cosas
la carne sin la palabra *carne*
o el ternero
sin su cuerpo frágil y tembloroso.

De tarde me recuesto en la cama.
Quiero dormir.
No puedo.
La voz de alguien resuena en mi mente
y eso no es carne.

VICTORIA ESTOL

translation by Seth Michelson

flesh and fingernail

i become again the cell that gave me life
i walk past the packets of sweetener you're not using
and lodge myself under the nail of your ring finger

i chew through your flesh, worm
carve your bone, termite
swim in your contradictory blood

against the current

i traverse your hippopotamus neck
scale your trachea
cut your vocal cords so you'll stop your speaking

arrive at your inner ear
scratch
slash your tympanic membrane

i fall in a crouch to the table and retake my seat
perch on my elbows on cold marble

and smile at you while i plot my coup.

carne y uña

me convierto en aquella célula que me dio origen
camino por los sobres del edulcorante que no vas a usar
y me meto justo debajo de tu uña del anular izquierdo

mastico tu carne, gusano
tallo tu hueso, termita
nado en tu sangre contradictoria

contracorriente

trepo tu cuello de hipopótamo
escalo tu tráquea
corto las cuerdas para que no hables más

llego a tu oído
araño
rajo tu tímpano

caigo en cuclillas sobre la mesa y vuelvo a mi asiento
apoyo los codos en el mármol frío

y te sonrío mientras planifico el golpe.

Airport

The bloodstain remains in the bathroom carpet. An owl at the ready, motionless, a daily reminder when they wake of what happened.

From an intense red it fades to dry brown.

She'd once tried to clean it. Dropped to her knees and scrubbed it till her bones ached, but failed.

Now she's heading to New York. In her carry-on she totes the book by Carver that he'd gifted to her. There's no dedication.

They did everything possible to avoid leaving tracks in each other's lives. Like two expert assassins, they erased every footprint, burned every clue.

He turned 45 degrees left. Found cloudless skies for his journey.

She'll never again wear high heels.

Aeropuerto

La mancha de sangre sigue en la alfombra del baño. Un búho al acecho, inmóvil, que les recuerda todos los días al levantarse lo que pasó.

Del rojo intenso pasó al marrón seco.

Ella intentó limpiarla una vez. Se arrodilló y cepilló hasta que le dolió el esqueleto, y no pudo.

Ahora se va a Nueva York. Guarda en el bolso de mano el libro de Carver que él le regaló. No tiene dedicatoria.

Hicieron todo lo posible para no dejar rastros en la vida del otro. Como dos perfectos asesinos borraron todas las huellas y quemaron las pistas.

Él giró 45 grados a la izquierda. Ahora tiene el paisaje más despejado.

Ella nunca volverá a usar tacos.

Untitled

Dearest,
Since we met I've been a red balloon filled with lead.
I want to negotiate.

I'm beginning to get what you want from me, but let's take it
    slow.
I believe in suicide attacks. *Ten cuidado.*

I like to dissect things, tweak a cable.
Put the heart in salt and see how long it beats.
Stretch vocal cords then flick them with my finger.
I rake fish scales backwards.
Roll eyes back in heads.

I throw my tentacles in the air. Fish come and go, I barely
    clench.
Even if the tide drops, I have plenty of water.

I'm a helium balloon filled with lead.
Let's negotiate.

Let's extract the lead and tie on a string, a long one.

Sin título

Estimado:
Desde que lo conocí soy un globo rojo con plomada adentro.
Quiero negociar.

Empiezo a entender lo que quiere de mí, pero vayamos
    despacio.
Yo sí creo en los hombres bomba. *Be careful.*

Me gusta disecar las cosas, tensar la piola.
Poner el corazón en sal y ver hasta cuando late.
Estirar las cuerdas vocales y darles un tiquiñazo.
Raspar escamas a contrapelo.
Al ojo, darlo vuelta.

Tiro tentáculos al aire. Los peces pueden entrar o salir, no
    aprieto mucho.
Si baja la marea, tengo agua suficiente.

Soy un globo de helio con plomada adentro.
Negociemos.

Saquemos la plomada y atemos una piola larga, muy larga.

minefield

by night they slip in through the cracks
begin their mission
the attack is noisy, hundreds of bites

i head for the kitchen parched
from the corner of my eye i see something not there
they devour my happiness

they carry off violet flowers among the many
hand them whole to their queen
the skeletal black shell

today combat erupts
powdered Raid lines my house
and i don boots.

campo minado

en la noche entran en tropa por mis rendijas
van directo al objetivo
el ataque es ruidoso, cientos de tarascones

sedienta voy a la cocina
por el rabo del ojo veo algo que no está
se devoran mi alegría

cargan entre varias las flores violetas
enteras se las regalan a su reina
esa esquelética coraza negra

hoy el combate se desata
Jimo en talco rodea mi casa
y visto botas.

Untitled

for Sam

two guys and me

we set the cans on fence posts
strung through their eyes with barbed wire
and count off 200 paces

they give it to me
it's heavy
i shoulder the weight
concentrate hard on the task at hand
focus

it's cold in my fingers
i fire
the kick bucks me
i fall

hit my head on a stone
staring up blind at the sky

the can
falls.

Sin título

para Sam

dos varones y yo

ubicamos las latas sobre los piques
por los ojos pasa el alambre de púas
caminamos 200 pasos

me la dan
pesa
la apoyo en el hombro
me concentro en la mira
focalizo

siento el frío en mis dedos
tiro
la descarga me empuja
caigo

la piedra se incrusta en mi cabeza
quedo ciega mirando al cielo

la lata
cae.

JAVIER ETCHEVARREN

translation by Don Bogen

Glue

always on the same corner
pablo relaxes with his plastic bag
shoulders defeated
eyes on loan
hands unrecognizable
legs subdued
pablo collapses with his plastic bag
while his neighbors blame the habit
while his mother lights candles for him
pablo gets lost with his plastic bag
antihunger pill
(after *mate* for lunch)
antiboredom stupefaction
(there's no future to make the present worth interest)
tragicomedy turned inward
unique self-torture
with a stunned smile and profound despair
that makes the plastic bag
more sticky every time

Pegamento

en la misma esquina de siempre
pablo descansa sobre su bolsa de nylon
espalda vencida
ojos prestados
manos irreconocibles
piernas sujetas
pablo se derrumba sobre su bolsa de nylon
mientras sus vecinos inculpan a la costumbre
mientras su madre enciende velas por él
pablo se pierde en su bolsa de nylon
píldora contra el hambre
(después de almorzar mate)
confusión contra el tedio
(no hay futuro que entusiasme al presente)
tragicomedia introspectiva
violento unipersonal
de risa alucinada y desdicha profunda
que cada vez lo tiene más adherido
a la bolsa de nylon

Punta Carretas

the prison is a shopping center now
that boutique was my cell
its plate glass windows my bars
I don't see the cattle prod among the electrical appliances
filthy rags aren't in fashion
the courtyard is easier to get to now it's a parking lot
the wall I used to talk with became an elevator
there's less damp, less mildew, less silence
and every day is visiting day

I love the way it smells now and all those open doors

the salesgirls are discussing
its plans for expansion
its sleazy eroticism
the distant smile in their eyes
with too much makeup
I hear one say
"Get me out of here!"
and it makes me sad

Punta Carretas

la cárcel es ahora un shopping center
aquella boutique fue mi celda
sus vitrinas mis rejas
no veo la picana entre los electrodomésticos
no están de moda los harapos pestilentes
es más accesible el patio ahora que es parking
la pared con la que dialogaba se hizo un lifting
hay menos humedad, moho, silencio
y todos los días son días de visita

me alegra su aroma actual y advertir tantas puertas abiertas

las promotoras conversan
con su esfuerzo por ser alta
con su erotismo prostituido
con la sonrisa alejada de sus ojos
con tantos maquillajes
escucho que una dice:
"¡qué ganas de irme!"
me entristezco

Lungs

the worn-out arteries of the city
spew copper
there are families who live off that death
they live in the toxic cloud
with no more protection than their skin
the metallic smoke strips away their profiles
a toxic shout deafens their sense of smell
and they live off that death
near a blaze of tires and rags
it's their job to gather up wire
at sunset other twilights take their toll
living off that death
they cough in their dinner plates when night comes
they'd like to remove
the copper that accumulates in their lungs
because it's worth eleven pesos a kilo
and these folks live off that death

Pulmones

las arterias caducas de la ciudad
derraman cobre
hay familias que viven de esa muerte
habitan la humareda tóxica
sin más resguardo que la piel
el vapor metálico les desagarra los perfiles
un grito tóxico ensordece los olfatos
y viven de esa muerte
con un fuego de neumáticos y harapos
obligan al cable a reunirse
tributan al ocaso otros crepúsculos
viviendo de esa muerte
llega la noche y tosen frente al plato de comida
quisieran arrancarse
el cobre que se acumula en los pulmones
porque lo pagan once pesos el kilo
y ellos viven de esa muerte

The Despicable Man Watching TV

it enters the eyes and comes out the mouth
a feed of words
to get our drives drooling
with exotic passions that sustain us
through the shock
of unending effluvium

everything happens at a distance
the despicable man
a parasite of circumstances
emperor of mediocrity

he has only himself for a family
he bangs into things
he abandons himself
watching TV

the screen is the horizon
the screen is the oracle we subscribe to
the screen is the answer when there are no questions

there is a place devoid of people
a feast gone rotten
an imaginary gift
there is love that accounts for the lechery
there is lechery that accounts for the place devoid of people

the despicable man watching TV
forfeiting the time he acquired at birth
a spectator excited by the show

Hombre vil frente a la televisión

entra por los ojos y sale por la boca
es una transmisión de verbos
para que nuestras pulsiones se saliven
en pasiones extrañas que sostenemos
al chocarnos con cualquiera
efluvio indiviso de la audiencia

todo acontece fuera de uno
parásito de las circunstancias
emperador de la mediocridad
hombre vil

él mismo es su familia
él mismo se golpea
él mismo se abandona
frente a la televisión

la pantalla es el horizonte
la pantalla es el oráculo para abonados
la pantalla es la respuesta cuando no hay preguntas

hay un lugar despoblado
un banquete putrefacto
un recuerdo imaginado
hay amor explicando la lujuria
hay lujuria explicando el lugar despoblado

hombre vil frente a la televisión
perdiendo el tiempo que ganó al nacer
espectador excitado de actuación

Garbage Dump

dessert for the starving
where there are people there's garbage
where there are people there's hope
including the hope to live off garbage

putrefaction central
surplus of misery
the despicable man is the celebrity of throwaways
appliances gone senile, the latest styles in shreds, storm clouds
    of plastic, maggot bonfire
to pass through life is to feed a garbage dump
laying out provisions
for an impoverished bacchanal

Basural

postre de la inanición
donde está el hombre hay basura
donde está el hombre hay esperanza
incluso de vivir de la basura

hogar de la putrefacción
exceso de la miseria
el hombre vil es la vedette de los desechos
artefactos seniles, jirones de moda, hoguera de larvas,
  nubarrones de plástico
transcurrir es alimentar un basural
como una fiesta
bacanal de la penuria

PAOLA GALLO

translation by Adam Giannelli

Words Like Knives

Promiscuous ruminant
go ahead already, now you know how to treat irreparable wrongs:
write.

Palabras como cuchillos

Promiscua rumiante
déjate ya, ahora sabes cómo curtir males irreparables:
escribe.

The Kiss

Asleep behind the rough fig
miraculous smiles:
surf of yellow scales, camouflage of fairies
in the sordid forest.

I have a foliage path about my face
a furtive worm's albino fuzz traces
in silken tingles aches of long ago.
In vertical vertigo shine
electric shocks:
map of concentric circles, barely enigma.

As in the painting by Klimt . . .
Strange proximity, two.

El beso

Detrás del áspero higo
dormitan sonrisas milagrosas:
oleaje de escamas amarillas, camuflaje de hadas
en el bosque sórdido.

Tengo un camino follaje por el rostro
gusano de tersa pelusa albina rastrea sigiloso
en sedoso cosquilleo dolores de antaño.
En vertical vértigo refulgen
descargas eléctricas:
mapa de círculos concéntricos, apenas enigma.

Como en el cuadro de Klimt. . .
Extraña cercanía, dos.

I Smell of "Amber Parenthesis"

> Sinister delirium to love a shadow.
> The shadow doesn't die.
> —ALEJANDRA PIZARNIK

Thirst and seduction
speak the same language,
scent of fresh flowers
     in the distance,
of spices in the hair.

You were delayed by the awakening from a murky dream.
Aquatic Ophelia, conspicuous vibration
anointing in abundance your own bones.

This poem is the wind arriving to air out the enclosures,
"wing of a cowardly bird," you call yourself, I call you wound,
   litany.

When you appeared the world stood steady,
a bottomless, lightless bloom:

there's no more thirst.
Although I suspect you're cyclical,
I won't wait for you anymore.

Huelo a "Ámbar Paréntesis"

> Siniestro delirio amar a una sombra.
> La sombra no muere.
> —ALEJANDRA PIZARNIK

La sed y la seducción
hablan un mismo idioma
olor a flores frescas
      a lo lejos,
a especias en el pelo.

Te detuvo el despertar de un sueño pastoso.
Acuática Ofelia, vibración untándote
conspicua en muchedumbre los huesos.

Este poema es el viento que llega para ventilar los encierros,
"ala de pájaro cobarde", así te llamas, te llamo herida, letanía.

Cuando asomaste se sostuvo el mundo,
desfondada floración sin luz:

no hay más sed.
Aunque te piense cíclica,
ya no te espero.

The Wave

I want to say what will never have words.
And always on another stage
—it's always another stage—
the unspeakable ebbs, pursuing an inviolable silence.

Between the fish bones and the weather you shoulder,
el darno explains: *throughout montevideo and its bitter sea.*

At forty, in foreign cities
    perhaps engrossed in writing's snare
    perhaps plump and contemplative in glasses
    looking for better images, simpler ones,
    more ambiguously elusive
    to say the same thing,
    and from afar
    always farther off and better said:

the fish bones and the weather you shoulder,
montevideo and its bitter sea.

Translator's note: "El Darno" is the nickname of Eduardo Darnauchans, an Uruguayan singer and songwriter. The italicized portion comes from his song "El ángel azul" (The Blue Angel), which alludes to Josef von Sternberg's film of the same name, starring Marlene Dietrich as Lola Lola, a cabaret headliner. The poem's title, "La ola," puns on Lola's name.

La ola

Quiero decir lo que nunca tendrá palabras.
Y siempre en otra escena
—siempre es en otra escena—
el reflujo de lo indecible persigue un silencio invicto.

Entre la espina y la intemperie a cuestas,
explica el darno: *por montevideo y su amargo mar.*

A los cuarenta, por ciudades ajenas
    quizá ensimismada en la trampa de la escritura
    quizá corpulenta y contemplativa con lentes
    buscando mejores imágenes, más simples,
    más ambiguamente esquivas
    para decir lo mismo,
    y desde lejos
    siempre más lejos y mejor dicho:

la espina y la intemperie a cuestas,
montevideo y su amargo mar.

Written from the Cave of the Predator

Although she hasn't yet been
the woman she will be
                          she suspects how much
it will cost to forget the word reminiscence.

That's why
on afternoons like this one she crafts a book like a tunnel
(through her)
she rubs the feverish spot on the brown girl's aquamarine dress,
she scratches the wet stone of the dark cave
in search of the sunlit
                    f
                    i
                    r
                    m
                    t
                    h
                    r
                    e
                    a
                    d

                A time tunnel
with red covers   and   bound pages.
Taut bow at rest where she, multiple, resides.

Escrito desde la cueva del depredador

Aunque todavía no ha sido
la mujer que será
                              sospecha cuánto
costará olvidar la palabra reminiscencia.

Por eso
en tardes como ésta fabrica un libro como túnel
(por ella)
restriega la afiebrada mancha en el vestido aguamarina de la
    niña marrón,
escarba la piedra húmeda de la negra cueva
buscando el soleado
                  h
                  i
                  l
                  o
                  r
                  í
                  g
                  i
                  d
                  o

           Un túnel de tiempo
con tapas rojas   y   páginas cosidas.
Tenso arco en reposo donde habitarse múltiple.

EL HOSKI (JOSÉ LUIS GADEA)

translation by Kevin González

Silence

the milky cock slams the table
        a mallet
the milky cock slams the table
oh   oh   oh
what is this I hear?
it is the poets
they beg for good words
and a rain of triangular dicks
that rains from the sky
        stars
insipid pills

silence I've said
allow the cock to express itself
milk
its boundless cavity
and the prostatic pains of the future
that will deny such an adjective

have I said adjective?
I have thousands of adjectives
asshole, piece of shit, cunt
grammar at the service of a good jerking off

but I do not see them quiet
silence goddamn it
a poet is speaking
his antennae erect towards the cosmos
the milky cock stirs
I'm coming can't stop
onomatopoeias
the milky cock slams the table
silence

Silencio

la pija lechosa golpea la mesa
        una maza
la pija lechosa golpea la mesa
oh   oh   oh
¿qué es eso que escucho?
son los poetas
me piden buenas palabras
y una lluvia de vergas triangulares
que llueve desde sobre el cielo
        estrellas
pepas insulsas

silencio he dicho
permitid que la pija se exprese
leche
su cavidad insondable
y la futura dolencia prostaica
que vendrá a desmentir tal adjetivo

adjetivo he dicho?
adjetivos tengo a miles
sorete, pedazo, conchuda
la gramática al servicio de una buena paja

pero no veo que se callen
silencio la reconcha de la madre
hay un poeta hablando
sus antenitas erectas al cosmos
la pija lechosa se agita
me acabo no aguanto
onomatopeyas
la pija lechosa golpea la mesa
silencio

Benedetti Is a Good Grampa

As a teen, I would sit on his lap
we brewed coffee and freebased
what a cock Mario had, what a poet

I remember my Soviet spy disguise
Mario would whip me
I was the Russian whore, the female slave
and he the soldier from Mississippi

(giddyup goes the red bull in the bullring
trip trap goes the trans-Siberian train
brimming with war prisoners
it holds up my cock
and the invited husky's as well)

Benedetti is a wise grandfather
how many intestinal mornings
how many comrades deceased
I would stroke his mustache
and suck on his dick

how great Benedetti was
the voice of the people
if only we could all be like him
what does the youth have?
their dick poems
a stuck turd where there's no ex-lax.

Benedetti es un abuelo bueno

me sentaba en su falda cuando era adolescente
hacíamos café con leche y fumábamos pasta
qué verga que tenía el Mario, qué poeta

recuerdo mi traje de espía soviética
Mario me azotaba
yo era la rusa, la puta, la esclava
él era el soldado de Misisipi

(arre caballa rojiza en el ruedo
arre con erre fecorrarril
transiberiano de prisioneros de guerra
soporta mi verga
y la del husky invitado también)

Benedetti es un abuelo sabio
cuántas mañanas de tripa
cuántos compañeros muertos
yo le atusaba el bigote
y le chupaba la pija

qué bueno era Benedetti
la voz del pueblo
ojalá todos fuésemos como Benedetti
¿qué les queda a los jóvenes?
los poemas de la pija
un sorete trancado sin actimel posible

On a Plane There Were

an Uruguayan a Brazilian
an Argentine a gazelle and a monkey
a pair of zebras
a chihuahua
three rhinos
a small elephant
and a chick that was still an egg
and a union member
and two racehorses
and a Facebook atheist
and two square dragons
     Moses
  an ark
and I'm missing two imbeciles
who hang from a tree
(who had not paid for their tickets)

and then one of the imbeciles
asks the camel:
how's your life going, man?
    humped
       humped
the dromedary responds

(Gol is a monster
a metal monster with a metal cock
and his balls are like soccer balls[1]
Gol's history is long
and it's the story of the first monster from Uruguay

---

[1]. "I have no strength to kick a ball; I just want to be beside you (chán, chán, chán). I'll die waiting for James Bond, for a miraaaaaaaaaaaaacle" (popular Russian song).

a boy and his father
listen to the game
and the old man explains everything:
the rules the insults
the custom of counting the nulled goals
    and the missed penalty kicks
of discounting the opponents' goals
    which were clearly offsides
one nil the boy says and smiles at the old man
it is the smoke from the grill
that rises triumphant in the memory of Sundays

but some small birds cannot be kept caged
their souls sadden and they refuse to sing
or at least they refuse to sing decent things
protoplanchas they become and wear Redondos T-shirts
    ten years Kbza, ten years without Peñarol winning the cup
    and the Three Kings who unexpectedly ceased visiting
become *protoplanchas* too and wear Iron Maiden T-shirts

and then the drugs
that, as I'm very original, it occurs to me
(as I am the Chirola, the cocksucker that sings in Hereford)
resemble women in the dependency they generate
in their confusion, in how necessary it is to eradicate them from
    Earth:
he took a spill heading toward forty
and almost without noticing wound up in the street

And then on a game day
our hero was strolling around Parque de los Aliados
Let's go el Manya let's go el Manya Let's go el Manya
and Peñarol still sucked
    how hungry I am!
and he began to eat from the trash

and he found a dumpster at the Hospital de Clínicas
full of radioactive products
and that's when he transformed

And like Frankenstein speaking to the girl from the lake
he approached an old lady at the bus stop
on the corner of avenida Italia
and screamed angrily at her left eyebrow
    I AM GOL
    I AM GOL
Gol is the first monster from Uruguay)

    Oh wait wait I forgot
then the other imbecile climbs down from the tree and asks the
    sound engineer:
the other day I listened to Genitales[2]
did you record them?

---

2. Genitales: Argentinian band from Morón, composed of Quieto Rodríguez (bassist for the Osos Greezly) and two anonymous sidekicks, which revolutionized *rioplatense* rock in the early '30s. They released two albums: *If You Don't Swallow, You Don't Love Me* and *The Vatican Should Release Flying Horses Instead of White Doves*. As was the case with the entirety of Generation Morón, the Genitales disappeared quickly, and their records have become inaccessible (*editor's note*).

Iban en un avión

un uruguayo un brasilero
un argentino una gacela y un mono
un par de cebras
un perro chihuahua
tres rinocerontes
un elefante chiquito
y un pollito que era huevo
y un sindicalista del SUNCA
y dos caballos de carrera
un ateo de los de Facebook
y dos dragones cuadrados
      Moisés
   un arca
y me faltan los dos soretes
que están colgados de un árbol
(que no habían pagado boleto)

y entonces uno de los soretes
le pregunta al camello:
¿cómo anda tu vida loco?
    jorobada
       jorobada
le contesta el dromedario

(Gol es un monstruo
un monstruo de metal con la pija de metal
y el par de huevos unidos semejando dos balones[1]
la historia de Gol es larga
y es la historia del primer monstruo uruguayo

---

1. "No tengo fuerzas pa' patear un balón; yo solo quiero estar junto a ti (chán, chán, chán). Moriré esperando que James Bond, que pase un milaaaaaaaaaaaaagro" (canción popular rusa).

un niño con su padre

están escuchando el partido
y el viejo le explica todo lo necesario:
las reglas las puteadas
el hábito de contar los goles anulados
    y los penales no cobrados
de descontar los goles rivales
    que se cometieron en orsaid
uno a cero corrobora y sonríe para su viejo es el humo del asado
que asciende jugoso en el recuerdo del domingo

pero algunos pajaritos no se pueden encerrar
se les va apenando el alma y de pronto ya no quieren cantar
o por lo menos no quieren cantar cosas decentes
en protoplanchas se convierten y usan remera de los Redondos
    diez años Kbza, diez años sin que Peñarol ganase una copa
      y los Reyes Magos que dejaron de venir inesperadamente
en protoplanchas se convierten y usan remera de Iron Maiden

y luego las drogas
que como a mí muy originalmente se me ocurre
(pues soy el Chirola, el chupaverga que canta en Hereford)
semejan a las mujeres en la dependencia que generan
en la confusión y en lo necesario que se hace erradicarlas del
   mundo:
se desparramó de a poco después que andaba por los cuarenta
y casi sin darse cuenta en la calle terminó

Y entonces un día de partido
nuestro héroe andaba por el parque de los Aliados
Vamo el Manya vamo el Manya Vamo el Manya
y Peñarol seguía sin ganar una mierda
    qué hambre que tengo
y se metió a comer de la basura
y agarró una volqueta en el fondo del Hospital de Clínicas

eran productos radiactivos
y entonces ahí se transformó

Y cual Frankenstein hablándole a la niña del lago
se acercó a una vieja que esperaba el 300
en la parada de avenida Italia
y le gritó enfurecido en medio de la ceja derecha
    YO SOY GOL
    YO SOL GOL
Gol es el primer monstruo uruguayo)

    ah pará pará me olvidaba
entonces el otro sorete se baja de la rama y le pregunta al sonidista:
el otro día escuché música de Genitales[2]
¿bo-las-grabaste?

---

2. Genitales: banda argentina originaria de Morón, que compuesta por el Quieto Rodríguez (bajista de los Osos Greezly) y otros dos compañeros anónimos de pabellón, supo revolucionar el ambiente rioplatense del rock a principios de los años 30. Llegaron a sacar dos álbumes: *Si no tragás no me querés* y *El vaticano debería soltar caballos voladores en vez de palomas blancas*. Como sucedió con la Generación Morón entera, los Genitales desaparecieron rápidamente, siendo imposible acceder hoy a alguno de sus DVDs (*nota del editor*).

LEONARDO LESCI
translation by Christopher Schafenacker

Río de la Plata

El río de la plata is low and I enter on its blind side,
the water drops
further still
like a woman penetrated by the steps of a bizarre dance.

El río de la plata is low and I walk up it.
I'd hoped to reach the axis of its two banks, I'd hoped to reach
    the river itself that
lies in the mud
maybe
in the mud

Rabid, I walk up along the sand toward the *nimble melody*
toward the sexual scrawling of shapes

The water gives way as if split by a man
a rudder made of flesh

the water recedes
but traces remain of what once was

el río de la plata is in the center because along its banks
el río de la plata is low

el río de la plata is an empty plate of sea

Lights emerge from the banks and confirm that we are in el Plata.
I will lie in this swamp for as long as it takes.

This is the logic of tango, I know, but not my reason for
    speaking.

A biologist from Buenos Aires once told me that el río de la
   plata was *an enormous basin*
of disgusting sediments
I listened and promised to stop writing *platense* poems.
I have since only spoken words that resound in puddles.
For example:
El río de la plata is low, and it wills me—rabid—to wade
until I am stuck in its mud, its sweet outskirts
and I enter on its blind side
stepping carefully into the night's murky silhouette
I enter
because the river is low
and the water gives way as if it were a woman ready to die.

Río de la Plata

El río de la plata está bajo, e ingreso en él por el lado ciego,
el agua merma
todavía más
como una mujer penetrada por los pasos de un baile bizarro.

El río de la plata está bajo, y por él avanzo.
Quisiera llegar al eje de las dos orillas, quisiera llegar al río
    mismo que
está en el barro
tal vez
en el barro

Rabiosamente avanzo por la arena hacia la *liviana melodía*
hacia el sexual garabato de las formas

El agua da paso como si fuese avanzada por un hombre
timonero de carne

el agua cada vez es menor
pero quedan indicios de que alguna vez estuvo

el río de la plata está en el centro porque en sus orillas
el río de la plata está bajo

el río de la plata es un plato vacío del mar

De las dos orillas surgen luces que confirman que estamos en el
    Plata.
Yaceré sobre ciénagas el tiempo que sea necesario.

Sé que esta es la lógica del tango pero yo hablo de otras razones.

Una bióloga porteña me dijo un día que el río de la plata era *una gran palangana de*
sedimentos asquerosos
Le hice caso. Prometí que no escribiría más poemas platenses.
Desde entonces solo digo palabras que retumban en un charco.
Por ejemplo:
El río de la plata está bajo y me alienta —rabioso —a caminar por él
hasta ser succionado en el lodo de sus dulces arrabales
y entro
por su lado ciego
con prolijos pasos a la silueta fangosa de la noche
y entro
porque el río está bajo
y el agua da paso como si fuese una mujer rendida ante la muerte.

Milonga–Folk-land

for F. L.

This poet's circle that looks south upon el Plata does not possess
   the origin.
It is a karaoke of clothing an industry of voices.

A succession of gauchos that face south
But
What is a gaucho?
An Italian in *bombachas* lives in Paysandú?
My *abuelo*? Maybe my *abuelo* was a gaucho . . . Am I the
   grandchild of a gaucho?
Or is it that Uruguay imported that creolized austral world as a
   way
of escaping the emptiness
the nothingness
of the great Antarctic gale that is this country,
our closest likeness the Falkland Islands
Uruguay's true neighbor

Who are they? Who were they?
I think they're Basque, Italian, Portuguese, German and perhaps
   a single Frenchmen,
just one
summed up
upon some Guarani brought in to cure meat and catch cannon
   balls.
They put on their *bombachas* and went to work: the rest is
   literature.
Books provided *plata* and an ethos
El Gaucho y La Moneda
and later, southern-cowboy movies consummated the situation

What difference is there between a gaucho and a German
 peasant,
their mouths sewn shut by the prairie cold?
Both are color and folklore.
Localized color upon our Babylonian bodies that beg to be
 looked at.

Milonga–Folk-land

a F. L.

Esta ronda de poetas que mira al sur por una ventana del Plata
   no posee el
origen.
Acaso sea un karaoke de vestidos una industria de la voz.

Una sucesión de gauchos que miran al sur
Pero
¿Qué es un gaucho?
Supongo que un italiano con bombachas que vive en Paysandú.
¿Qué es un gaucho?
¿Mi abuelo? Acaso mi abuelo era un gaucho. . . ¿Soy nieto de los
   gauchos?
O será que Uruguay importó el mundo criollo austral como una
   forma de no
sentir el vacío
de la nada
del gran vendaval antártico que es este país,
nuestro verdadero vecino son las Falkland Islands
lo más parecido a Uruguay

¿Quiénes son? ¿Quiénes fueron?
Pienso que son vascos, italianos, portugueses, alemanes y quizá
   un francés, sólo
uno
sumados
a algún guaraní traído para el tasajo de la carne como carne de
   cañón.
Se pusieron bombachas para las tareas de fajina: lo demás es
   literatura.
La literatura les entregó un ethos y también la plata
el gaucho y la moneda
y luego el cine con sus *cow boys* del sur consumó la situación

¿Qué diferencia hay entre un gaucho y un campesino alemán cuando el frío de la
pradera les cose la boca?
Ambos son color y folklore.
Localizado color en el cuerpo babilónico con que gusta que nos miren.

river plate fresh meat company

We've seen your cow next to a river that wasn't green

nor red
nor yellow
a fractured and imprecise river
a politically tinted river of interchangeable flags

the cow you spoke of in your Republic was expelled like a
   poet . . .

left a void in the pasture that was filled by a eucalyptus
(those trees that provide shade in proportion to their size)
left a void in the pasture
(like a wake in the sea)
a void in the pasture.

I want a cow between your pages a cow
to appear stammering between your pages.
Because
the cows that you kill—papyrusly—are in good health.

river plate fresh meat company

Hemos visto la vaca que querías junto a un río que no era verde
   ni
colorado
ni amarillo
un río desgarrado e impreciso
un río de colores políticos con banderas que cambiaron sus
   colores

la vaca que pronunciaste en tu República fue expulsada como
   un poeta. . .

dejó un vacío en la pradera que fue ocupado por eucaliptos
(estos árboles dan sombra en forma proporcional al tamaño con
   el que crecen)
dejó un vacío en la pradera
(como estelas en el mar)
un vacío en la pradera.

Quiero una vaca entre tus papeles que aparezca una vaca
   tartamudeando entre tus papeles.
Porque
las vacas que vos matás —papíricamente— gozan de buena salud.

Saltwater River

This stain in the ocean that we call a river
was traversed along its shallows by silver-plated Vikings
a stripe, red or bloody
in the water.

The muse caged in the river's belly sings the song of the sea.
A river drowned in a highway of salt
A river bristling like the music's sad bellows—aerial—when it
   plays its last.

All of these metaphors succeed at giving us a name
but none provide the precise form, the mud that will never dry.

This stain in the ocean that we call a river is the perpetual light
   of our dark lake.

Río salado

Esta mancha en el océano que llamamos río
fue cruzada en sus veriles por vikingos de plata
una franja roja o de sangre
en el agua.

La musa acorralada en el estómago del río es música del mar.
Un río ahogado en una autopista de sal
Un río erizado como el fuelle triste de la música cuando —aérea
 —la voz tocó su fin.

Son todas estas metáforas más o menos exitosas las que nos dan
 un nombre y
por el cual respondemos. Pero ninguna nos devuelve la forma
 exacta. Es un
barro que jamás habrá de secarse.

Esta mancha en el océano que llamamos río también es la luz
 perpetua del lago oscuro.

Thalweg

We might then say that *the valley path* is the most just.
The true thalweg runs beneath the water.
Because justice is buried deep in the earth's strata.

An extensive literature of names precedes us.
A fluvial ocean, an estuary, a bay, a mighty confluence, a historic
    inlet.
A freshwater sea
A saltwater river.

None of these names will return life to those bodies
when the Plata's transitory nature reveals their ashes.

Neither the zones of exclusive jurisdiction nor the common
    navigable waterways
will matter when a delta of terms deposits truth in the confused
    salt
of the sea.

There is an invisible riverbank between our two countries an
    aquatic calligraphy that defines us.

Thalweg

Entonces diremos que tal vez *el camino del valle* sea el más justo.
El verdadero *thalweg* se encuentra bajo las aguas.
Porque bajo las aguas la justicia es profunda en las capas de la tierra.

Una extensa literatura de frases y nombres nos precede.
Un río mar, un estuario, una bahía histórica, una barra de grandes ríos, un mar
cerrado, un río oceánico.
Un mar dulce
Un río salado.

Ninguno de estos nombres le devolverá la vida a los cuerpos cuando la
naturaleza transitoria del Plata revele sus cenizas.

Tampoco importarán las franjas de jurisdicción exclusivas ni las aguas comunes
de navegación cuando un delta de nombres deposite la verdad en la sal confusa
del océano.

Hay una ribera invisible en los dos países una caligrafía acuática nos define.

AGUSTÍN LUCAS

translation by Jesse Lee Kercheval

Plaza de los Bomberos

Plaza de los Bomberos, eleven in the morning, constantly crossed by everyone, constantly flown over by pigeons, watched over by the yawns of the firemen's barracks and by the statue of Lavalleja on his horse: indecisive, insecure . . . too pensive to take a step. Hard cold.

The suit jackets and the trench coats hurry on their way, stylish glasses cross paths, check each other out. Children pass the time with their grandmothers, the grandmothers pass the time with their scarves and their regrets.

The homeless men in the social club under the trees laugh and chat: "Bring me a cigarette!" they shout at whoever moves himself to take an unexpected turn around the plaza.

Today the shelter, that inn where they meet, waits almost in silence. The wind whistles between them until that sound is interrupted, as it often is, by the sharp tapping of high heels wanting to pass: a brief hush falls over the club. The youngest takes off his cap, kindly steps to one side with a bow; the women in high heels does not even look at him as she cautiously descends the stairs. Away she goes with her anger and her insolence, and the men return to being sentinels of the morning.

In the club, they know the bad moods of Mondays, there are no rules of admission nor opening or closing hours, they respect the people, and they share their bread with the dogs, as well as the pigeons that fight with the skillful sparrows over the sky and the crumbs, that play with the streams of the fountain, breaking their picture-perfect monotony, then fly in large circles, parting the cold as far as the indecision of Lavalleja and his horse. From there, they observe the plaza, mistresses of winter.

In the plaza the approximately twenty green benches are occupied by approximately twenty people: I am one of them. Only two veterans share one bench, exchange words once in a while, adjust their berets and smoke the apparent peace of retirement.

In front of me, a stranger receives another stranger. Their style of greeting is a nod of the head. The one who was already occupying the bench looks, perplexed, at the newly arrived man a few seconds, guards his breakfast, gathers himself up, then goes in search of another uncomfortable improvised dining room. The other looks, perplexed, at the deserter, clucks his tongue, then accepts the accustomed solitude.

Someone asks me permission to sit down. She is a lady of about sixty years who seems to think violet is in fashion, with a cell phone sounding a mechanized version of the tango "Cumparsita" in rising volume while she searches for it in her purse.

"Yes, I've been paid already! Yes!" she shouts as if the person on the phone were on the other side of the plaza.

I look at her and think, "You, too, understand only a little about those things that no one understands."

In the living room of the club, the wooden benches form an L so everyone can see one another's faces: today, the faces are complaining. The stairs seem to be more comfortable, and some are stretched along them. A man lies down on one of the free benches and falls asleep; another gives him a look and reminds him that is his place for the night, that these are his things, his dinner and his knife: the other doesn't answer and surrenders to a nap, to the little sun full of winter.

The carpet of grass and ground is populated by papers and journals, cardboard boxes for the night, clothes and bags. Crowds of women pass at lunch hour. Some are good-looking; the others are good-looking too. That madman continues to argue with the wood of the bench, alone, observed, immunized.

Images are projected rapidly across corneas, again and again, familiar people, the madman, the club, women, men, trench coats, the woman in violet, me, noon: *12:00* scolded the digital clock. I should go, too. I forsake my companion. I will leave her to occupy this bench in solitude: one of the approximately twenty benches occupied by approximately twenty people. She is one of many, sitting on two planks of wood screwed to eternal iron. Near the club, brushed by the cries of the market, guest of unexpected friends, alone, with her crochet and her needles, with her phone, her deafness, and her scarf.

Plaza de los bomberos

Plaza de los bomberos, once de la mañana: constantemente transitada por todos, constantemente sobrevolada por las palomas, custodiada por los bostezos del cuartel de bomberos y por Lavalleja en su caballo: indeciso, inseguro. . . demasiado pensativo a dar el paso. Duro de frío.

Los sacos y las gabardinas se apuran, los lentes de moda se cruzan, se miran. Los niños pasan las horas con sus abuelas, las abuelas pasan las horas con sus bufandas y sus vergüenzas.

Los hombres de la calle en el club social bajo de los árboles ríen y conversan:
—¡Trae un cigarro! —le gritan a quién se movió tras una fortuita vuelta a la plaza.

Ahora la morada, aquella posada de encuentro, aguarda casi en silencio. Entre ellos surca el viento libre hasta que interrumpe otra vez, como tantas, el taconeo seco que intenta pasar: se silencia aún más la escasa charla del club. El más joven acomoda su gorra y amablemente se hace a un lado con una reverencia; la mujer de los tacos ni lo mira y desciende con cuidado el escalón. Allá se va con su enfado e insolencia, y los hombres todos vuelven a ser centinelas de la mañana.

En el club se conocen los malhumores del lunes, no hay derecho de admisión ni hora de entrada o salida, se respeta a la gente, y a los perros se los convida del pan, como a las palomas: estas palomas disputan el cielo y las migas con los hábiles gorriones, juegan con los hilos de la fuente sacudiendo lo pintoresco de su monotonía, y vuelan al fin largas carreras partiendo al frío hasta la indecisión de Lavalleja y su caballo. Desde allí observan la plaza, amas del invierno.

Los aproximadamente veinte bancos verdes son ocupados por los aproximadamente veinte humanos: yo soy uno de estos tantos. Tan solo dos veteranos comparten el asiento, intercambian de vez en cuando algunas palabras, acomodan sus boinas y pitan la aparente paz de una jubilación.

Enfrente un desconocido recibe a otro desconocido. A modo de saludo asienten con la cabeza. Quién ya ocupaba el asiento mira perplejo al recién llegado unos segundos, guarda su desayuno, se acomoda y se va en busca de otro inhóspito comedor improvisado. El otro mira perplejo al desertor, chista desaprobación y se presta acostumbrado a la soledad.

Alguien me pide permiso. Es una señora de unos sesenta años que parece estar a la moda con el violeta, con su celular intentando una "Cumparsita" mecanizada subiendo de volumen mientras busca en la cartera.

¡Sí, ya cobré sí! —grita como si el otro estuviese del otro lado de la plaza.

La miro y pienso, "Usted también entiende poco algunas cosas que no se entienden."

En el living del club los bancos de madera forman una ele para verse las caras: las caras de hoy están como quejándose. Las escaleras parecen el lugar más cómodo, y algunos están tirados a lo largo de ellas. Uno se recuesta en uno (de los bancos sueltos) y se presta al sueño; hay otro que enseguida lo mira y le recuerda que ese es su lugar para la noche, que allí están sus cosas, su cena y su cuchillo: el otro no contesta y se entrega a la siesta, al solcito lleno de invierno.

La alfombra de pasto y tierra se puebla de papeles y diarios, cartones para la noche, ropas y bolsas. Pasan un montón de mujeres a la hora del almuerzo. Las algunas son bonitas, las otras también son bonitas. Aquel loco continúa discutiendo con las maderas del banco, sólo, observado, inmunizado.

Las imágenes se proyectan rápidas sobre las córneas, repetidas, conocidas, el loco, las mujeres, el club, los hombres, las gabardinas, la señora, yo, el mediodía: LAS DOCE rezongó el aviso digital. Yo también debo irme. Abandonaré a mi acompañante, la dejaré ocupar en soledad este banco: uno de los aproximadamente veinte bancos que ocupan las aproximadamente veinte personas. Ella es una de esas tantas, recostada sobre los dos metros de tablas de madera atornilladas al eterno hierro. Cerca del club, rozada por los gritos de la feria, convidada de amigos repentinos, sola, con su crochet y sus agujas, con su teléfono, su sordera y su bufanda.

General Flores without Flowers

Avenida General Flores is beautiful in the nights so late they are early Monday mornings, with traffic lights red, then green, with the customary desolation and mystery in its side streets.

General Flores in watchfulness, watching autumn hesitate with dead leaves on this paradise of cement and stone, of plastic and wood furniture for sale.

The corner with Blandengues is entangled with the wind in a relentless whirl of one-way streets; the bus terminal, abandoned, transformed, melancholic: the melancholy that lies alone, forgotten, incapable on the platforms occupied last Sunday by drums and boys, competing with the litany of seven o'clock.

The Terminal Goes, Marcelino Sosa Street covering its back: quick, attentive, dark; the community center and library, the posters, the sidewalks, the wind revolving in the bars.

Transients take short strolls along the sidewalks, characters that remain nameless for all time, and from the city buses, faces shout against sleep, blinking at the stops, are surprised by the rain or leave dirty images to be washed away by the drops on the windows. The transients outside also get soaked.

The dirt of some flower bed splashes mud on the clay pots. The desolation is implacable and is not disturbed by the lost whistle that warns of who comes or goes, feels or thinks, sings or hums the sadness of a tango with dark circles under his eyes. Then the novelty dance happens, the loneliness that sings in the instant when lovers are left at their doors. Not engines, nor the horns when a 169 and a 505 cross, not the bottles that roll, not the bells, not any of these sonorous events, not what will be seen falling down on the inhospitable street, will disturb the inclement desolation of the avenue, home of whores and transvestites, of worker and neighbor, of dealer and crackhead on the corners.

The transients sleep, children of the street, with one eye obviously open, the proprietors of the stairs and of the railing, of the glass, of the bottle, of the remains of noodles and the heels of bread, of the blanket and the flip-flops, of the size extra large, or of the toes sticking out. Prisoners of winter, free of the calendar and of the clock, heroes of the tranquility, friends of the dogs.

Transients stroll, return, leave, transients buy, sell, leave, transients keep watch, transients rave, stop, begin again, leave, transients believe, transients steal, leave, transients create, cry, deceive, transients lose, win, leave.

General Flores walks in its sleep, and the furniture and the prices quiet down even more, and the beds cool down even more, the plazas and seductive shop windows lower the voltage of the lights, until it is sparkling, dry, free of shadow plays.

General sin flores

Es tan bella General Flores en las altas madrugadas de los bajos lunes, con sus luces rojas y ahora verdes, con la corriente desolación y el misterio en sus bocacalles.

General Flores en vigilia, vigila lo que vacila el otoño con las hojas muertas del paraíso de cemento y piedra, de plástico y madera de muebles en venta.

La esquina con Blandengues se enreda con el viento en un implacable remolino del calles flechadas; la terminal de ómnibus, abandonada, transformada, melancólica: la melancolía sola, olvidada, yace incapaz en los andenes ocupados por tambores y gurises del ayer domingo, lidiando la letanía de la hora 19.

La terminal Goes, Marcelino Sosa cubriendo las espaldas: rápida, atenta, oscura; el comunal y la biblioteca, los afiches, las veredas, el viento revoleando de los bares.

Transeúntes se pasean escasos por las veredas, personajes innominados por el tiempo, y desde el transporte capitalino las caras vociferan contra el sueño, guiñan las paradas, se extrañan ante la lluvia o se dejan mojar la imagen sucia que gotea las ventanas. Los transeúntes afuera, también se mojan.

La tierra de algún cantero salpica de barro los ladrillos de la maceta. La desolación se vuelve implacable, y no la perturba el silbido perdido que avisa que viene o que va, que siente o que piensa, que canta o tararea la tristeza de un tango con ojeras. La novedad bailable que acontezca, la soledad que canta al instante cuando se dejan los enamorados en las puertas. Ni los motores, ni la bocina que cruzan en un 169 y un 505, ni las botellas que ruedan, ni los timbres, ni estos sonoros aconteceres, ni los que verá caer la inhóspita calle, perturbará la inclemente desolación de la avenida, morada de putas y travestis, de obrero y vecino, de transa y latero en las esquinas.

Los transeúntes duermen, hijos de la calle, con evidente ojo abierto, dueños del escalón y de la reja, del vaso, de la botella, del resto de fideos y el codo del pan, de la frazada y la chancleta, del talle grande, o de los dedos para afuera. Presos del invierno, libres del calendario y del reloj, héroes del sosiego, amigos de los perros.

Transeúnte pasea, vuelve, se va, transeúnte transa, vende, se va, transeúnte campana, transeúnte delira, cesa, vuelve, se va, transeúnte trata, cree, transeúnte roba, se va, transeúnte crea, llora, engaña, transeúnte pierde, gana, se va.

Gral. Flores reposa deambulada, y se aquietan aún más los muebles y los precios, y se enfrían aún más las camas, las plazas, y se bajan las tensiones de las luces vidrieras seductoras, tintineantes, secas, sin juego chino de sombras.

The Hour of the Birds

for Joaquín

The hardware store and the warehouse open.
The woman selling vegetables is looking strong.
You keep spinning around.
You. Her.
You walk through the barrio stinking of pain.
Your mouth lets out a mocking tone.
No matter that from the balcony
all that hangs is a feeling.
You leave it hanging.
A tile a hole a bottle a dog
you kick or dodge everything without thinking.
You are the Ronaldinho of rock 'n' roll,
you have the tight dribbling of a man who just left a bar,
the mark, man to man, is on you,
the certain shot on the edge of superego.
A short touch of whiskey without ice.
A long pull
of love.

La hora de los pájaros

para Joaquín

Abrió la ferretería y el almacén.
La verdulera está fuerte.
Vos seguís girando alrededor.
De vos. De ella.
Paseás por el barrio hediondo a dolor.
Tu boca se pianta en tono burlón.
No importa que del balcón
sólo cuelgue una sensación.
La dejás colgada.
Una baldosa un pozo una botella un perro,
todo lo pateás y lo eludís sin discreción.
Sos el Ronaldinho del rocanrol,
tenés el dribling justo del mostrador,
la marca hombre a hombre está sobre vos,
disparo certero al borde del súper yo.
Toque corto de whisky sin hielo.
Saque largo
del amor.

River Runs

I am entering the barrio,
people are sitting outside
smoking, hoping
that it rains.
I go deep into the barrio,
cobblestones, a thousand springtimes,
secret wandering strides,
the barrio made poem.
Lightning from the storm
merges with the shadows.
Future ex-con on the corner
blends *cumbia* with old tango,
in the background the smell of weed.
Smell of weeds and earth.
Three fireworks
part the cloud in two,
I do not have an umbrella nor have I ever.
The sidewalk
takes care of me.

Río va

Voy entrando en el barrio,
la gente sentada afuera
fumando espera
que llueva.
Me voy adentrando al barrio,
adoquines, mil primaveras.
Sigiloso tranco errante,
el barrio hecho un poema,
se confunden con las sombras,
refucilos de tormenta.
Plancha conjuga en la esquina
con cumbia, milonga vieja,
de fondo olor a hierba.
Olor a hierba y a tierra.
Tres fuegos artificiales,
parten en dos una nube,
no tengo paraguas ni tuve
de mí se encarga
la vereda.

ELISA MASTROMATTEO
translation by Orlando Ricardo Menes

As Simple as That

One must simply
let it
come out, one must let it
it wants to come out, and it goes forth
forges new energies
comes out, breathes
rummages through objects, removes lint
it looks and points, makes drawings
leaps a bit
and later gets lost.

Or it comes back
to once again
be transformed.

Tan simple como eso

Hay que dejar
que salga
simplemente, hay que dejarlo
quiere salir y va
forja energías nuevas
sale, respira
revuelve objetos, quita pelusas
mira y señala, hace dibujos
salta un rato
después se pierde.

O regresa
para nuevamente
ser transformado.

Game

Almost always, or indeed always,
his surrender was absolute.
A body and its space,
both
whirling, making, coming out.
The hands pressing against
the lukewarm silence.
The air penetrating itself,
the silhouette.
Simple and at the same time complex,
your manner
of murmuring by shuddering
of whistling by shaking
of flying by alternating
elbows and feet.
And almost always, or indeed always,
your eyes being life itself,
your soul so present.

Juego

Y casi siempre, o siempre
la entrega era total.
Un cuerpo y su espacio,
ambos
girando, haciendo, saliendo.
Las manos apremiando el tibio silencio.
El aire internándose,
la silueta.
Simple y a la vez compleja
tu manera
de murmurar estremeciendo
de silbar meneando
de volar alternando
codos y pies.
Y casi siempre, o siempre
tus ojos siendo vida
tu alma tan presente.

That

It is true.
It may be
a continuous illusion an infinite beginning
an internal journey to discover
new things
stones once invisible
fire behind the stones
tremors falls pains
and recently behind
behind all of this
warmth and equilibrium, happiness.
But it is true.
It is true, and it exists.
Perhaps by accident, but why does it matter.
It is ours,
and that is it.

Eso

Es verdad.
Puede que sea
una ilusión continua un infinito comienzo
un recorrido interno descubriendo
cosas nuevas
piedras antes invisibles
fuego detrás de las piedras
temblores caídas dolores
y detrás
recién detrás de todo eso
tibieza y equilibrio, felicidad.
Pero es verdad.
Es verdad y existe.
Y tal vez por accidente, qué importa.
Es nuestro
y es ya.

A Before

When did I come back?
Really, when?
I am here seated
surrounded by familiar things.
I would affirm:
this is my garden
or my street.
Without a doubt
it is *my place*.
But waiting so long for that girl
to return with me,
what happened to the road?
And all those stories
that I know she told me
know that we talked so much
know which words
and which smile.
I know, too, which colorful fairies
and which made-up worlds.
I know everything or maybe just knew
I doubt myself because I still
cannot remember
our way back.

Un antes

¿Cuándo volví?
En serio, ¿cuándo?
Acá estoy sentada
rodeada de cosas familiares.
Yo afirmaría:
es este mi jardín
o mi calle.
Es sin dudas
un mi lugar.
Pero esperar tanto aquella niña
para que vuelva conmigo
¿qué pasó con el camino?
Y con las historias
que sé que me contó
sé que hablábamos tanto
sé que palabras
y que sonrisas.
Sé también que hadas de colores
y que mundos inventados.
Sé todo o sabía
es que dudo, porque no logro
no puedo recordar
todavía
nuestro camino de vuelta.

Hideout

We had to get out
run
get on the first bus
and fly
or not,
but get out.
Grab all the most
precious things
or the things will simply
go after us,
because over there
we will not take care of things
it is not necessary there
to keep anything under key
we will go there
to save ourselves.

Yes, ourselves.
From the world.

Escondite

Había que salir
había que correr
subirse al primer ómnibus
y volar
o no,
pero salir.
Agarrar todas las cosas
más preciadas
o las cosas simplemente
irán tras nosotros,
porque allá no cuidaremos
allá no se precisa
guardar nada bajo llave
allá iremos
para guardarnos nosotros.

Sí, nosotros.
Del mundo.

ALEX PIPERNO

translation by Vicente Marcos López Abad

from *Sahara*

1.

a collection of girls full of shoulder blades sleeps structure of dog listen to the rattling of their back when they twist or switch sides insist on a punctuality that falls from its eyes.

2.

a collection of small figures gets pregnant at an astonishing speed the figures have the shape of the star of david structure of dog listen to the rattling of their points when they twist insist on a punctuality that falls from its eyes.

3.

a collection of girls without shoulders lets their skin grow yellow until they are shifted somewhere else.

4.

a collection of transparent and portable stones turns acidic like a string of garlic in the crotch of girls with a family vocation.

5.

a collection of girls with punctuality gets pregnant automatically the rattling of the heads of the king children fills their eyes with tears.

6.

a ballet of instant children enters a machine to get little figures pregnant at an astonishing speed.

7.

a prosthesis that puts me to work as a dog-sterilizer lady of automatic animals.

8.

balter ölhms delivers a package of sons to the ambassador so she will smoke them with lots of feelings.

9.

instructions to become clumsy and hairy hammocks.

10.

the ambassador opens up like a really old fridge really old girl exits the war girl stalin propensity to getting myself shot.

de *Sahara*

1.

una colección de muchachas llenas de omóplatos duerme estructura de perro escucha el golpeteo de sus espaldas cuando giran o cambian de lado insiste en una puntualidad que se le cae de los ojos.

2.

una colección de figuras pequeñas se embaraza a velocidades asombrosas las figuras tienen forma de estrella de david estructura de perro escucha el golpeteo de sus puntas cuando giran insiste en una puntualidad que se le cae de los ojos.

3.

una colección de muchachas sin hombros deja que la piel se les ponga amarilla hasta que las corran de lugar.

4.

una colección de piedras transparentes y portátiles se pone ácida como una ristra de ajos en las entrepiernas de muchachas con vocación familiar.

5.

una colección de muchachas con puntualidad se embaraza automáticamente el golpeteo de las cabezas de los niños rey les llena los ojos de lágrimas.

6.

un ballet de niños prontos entra a una máquina de embarazar figuras pequeñas a velocidades asombrosas.

7.

una prótesis de ponerme a funcionar como un castra perros señora de animales automáticos.

8.

balter ölhms entrega a embajadora un paquete de hijos machos para que se los fume con muchos sentimientos.

9.

instrucciones para convertirse en hamacas torpes y peludas.

10.

embajadora se abre como una heladera muy antigua muchacha muy antigua sale de la guerra muchacha stalin manía de querer hacerme fusilar.

Colony

we fall into a dream embracing valentina's feet and in her dream
   we are a small house a
collection of engineers who design a cybele trapping system in her
   stomach an
antigravitational train engine a brush that strokes a pubis

it was said in whispers that the landscape works and adds parts to
   itself over the silent rhythm of a crank turning

it was said let's unfold a grassland with broken animals and let's
   place them in valentina's
dream so she will remain trapped in her own lucidity and never
   come back

then you came out of the grasslands asleep like a cart

with a basket full of hells that you started placing into demijohns
   and then
selling them off in the valley

a grassland unfolds like a sudden hell throughout the lengths of
   the valley which were just like
tiny coffers and from within pocket-sized engineers spring up and
   start conquering everything

and they start burning everything because the island followed its
   spirit never expecting things to stay in place

the wrecked lung motors of little girls of milk whisper words into
   valentina's ear you return from
the grasslands in love with death because the expired potatoes
   sprout up from
the earth everywhere

like a symbol which is entirely false if in the harbor everyone was
    delighted to be there and
no one was being up-front with you valentina and we'd tie ribbons
    on our arms to please you

and straight away you rushed into the thicket of my shoulder and
    then we ran together

we woke up in the grasslands every morning we tear off some
    leaves and eat them
with fruit michel brought chops of electrocuted animals that we
    also ate

while he comes back he says smiling it seems as though they were
    precooked then from the pocket
of his t-shirt a branch grows which is the savage genealogy of the
    king children and the hard cores
of the king children start dropping down like potatoes

michel comes back with the jungle sticking out of his pocket and
    the jungle is a hanger that bears the
history of the king children that sprout one day like girls from the
    depths of the valley

the first potato is alejo's head which is staring at me with slanted
    and piercing eyes

the prime potato with alberto's blue eyes showing under the ski
    mask

oscar and abraham's heads are two potatoes that arrived stuck
    together from the war laurita's
potato shines like a relic that fell out of a pocket and immediately
    disappears into the clouds

the vegetal nucleus of guillermo's head didn't have a face and it
    questioned us extraordinarily
its fall drew a groan from the island's center that woke everyone
    up

and the clouds made it be known that inside the potatoes there
    were information pills and
more than three hundred males with crowns had been crawling
    across the grasslands

valentina and I stare at the sprouting as we can with our teeth lost
    in the thighs of
the animals and our hands doused in fat

Colonia

nos dormimos abrazados a los pies de valentina y en su sueño somos una casa chica una
colección de ingenieros que diseñan un sistema en su estómago para atrapar cibeles una
locomotora antigravitatoria un pincelito que se pasa por el pubis

se dijo en susurros el paisaje trabaja y se va agregando partes a sí mismo al ritmo silencioso de una manivela

se dijo despleguemos un pastizal con animales destrozados y coloquémoslo en el sueño de
valentina para que se quede trancada en su lucidez propia y no regrese nunca

entonces saliste de los pastizales dormida como una carreta

con la canasta llena de infiernos que los ibas poniendo adentro de damajuanas y después los
vendías en el valle

un pastizal se despliega como un infierno sorpresa por las extensiones del valle que eran como
cofrecitos de madera y de adentro salen pequeños ingenieros que van conquistando todo

y van quemando todo porque la isla funcionaba en su ánimo de no esperarle cosas en su sitio

los pulmotores destrozados de las pequeñas de leche le susurran a valentina cosas al oído de
los pastizales saliste enamorada de la muerte por todos lados saltan papas vencidas de
abajo de la tierra

como un símbolo que es completamente falso si en el puerto estábamos todos encantados y
ninguno hablaba en serio contigo valentina y nos atábamos cintas a los brazos para ilusionarte

y enseguida corriste a internarte adentro de mi hombro y entonces yo también corrí contigo

despertábamos en los pastizales todas las mañanas arrancamos algunas hojas y las comemos
con fruta michel trajo pedazos de animales electrocutados que también comimos

mientras vuelve dice sonriendo parece que ya vienen cocinados de antes entonces del bolsillo
de su remera crece una rama que es la genealogía salvaje de los niños rey y los núcleos duros
de los niños rey empiezan a caerse como papas

michel vuelve con la selva saliéndole del bolsillo y la selva es una percha de la que cuelga la
historia de los niños rey que brotan como niñas desde el fondo del valle

la primera papa es la cabeza de alejo que me mira con los ojos achinados y agudos

la primicia papa con los ojos azules de alberto por abajo del pasamontañas

la cabeza de abraham y óscar son dos papas que vinieron pegadas de la guerra la papa de
laurita brilla como una reliquia que se soltó del bolsillo y enseguida desaparece entre las nubes

el núcleo vegetal la cabeza de guillermo no llevaba rostro y nos interpeló de una manera
extraordinaria su caída provocó un quejido en el centro de la isla que despertó a todos

y las nubes mandaron a decir que adentro de las papas había cápsulas con informaciones y
más de trescientos varones con coronas que venían pegados a unos pastizales

valentina y yo miramos el broterío como podemos con los dientes perdidos en los muslos de
los animales y tenemos las manos llenas de grasa

from "the lovers"

I.
A river of vertical foam legless an old
colored adam and in slow motion
the towers the chimneys the trains from edge
to edge the coat hanger next to the door
to hang the hat the briefcase and my
adorable wife's kisses the convex
mirrors the thirty centimeter
ruler that is twenty centimeters long
the propagandas the white water
trying to climb up the knee he makes
believe nothing is going on he says he is
a river of vertical foam legless
she is almost a river too but sometimes
she speaks the truth.

de "los amantes"

I.
un río de espuma vertical sin piernas un
adán de colores viejo y en ralenti las
torres las chimeneas los trenes de arista
a arista el perchero al lado de la puerta
para dejar el sombrero el portafolio y los
besos de mi adorable esposa los espejos
convexos las reglas de treinta
centímetros que miden veinte centímetros
las propagandas el agua blanca tratando
de subir por las rodillas él hace de
cuenta que no pasa nada él dice que es
un río de espuma vertical sin piernas
ella también es casi un río pero a veces
dice la verdad.

from "ars poetica two"

I.
From not saying zilch to garter belt
of sharp wires our legs ground meat like
lepers in feminine proportions never
such beauty thrown together on the floor
let's go pick it up with pots or shovels
god it's true there is nobody the
studs on the point of the foot the sole
stuck to the flesh that was a leg and now
is white spotted meat the sound that
takes off and walks the stave of
death a haughty comedy the resounding
vivid crimson carpet the liquid carpet
the textured tongue the ten-seater sofa
on the sofa another body seated the smell
traversing it yellow from head to toe
the mandatory clothing I thought it was
brazilian modernism but it's only a
leg.

de "ars poetica dos"

I.
de no decir nada a portaligas de alambre
filoso las piernas como carne picada la
lepra en proporciones femeninas nunca
tanta belleza junta tirada en el suelo
vayamos con palas o cacerolas a
recogerla dios es verdad no hay nadie los
tacos en la punta la suela adherida carne
que supo ser pierna y que ahora es carne
con manchas blancas el sonido se
despega y camina un pentagrama de
muerte una comedia soberbia la alfombra
sonora color carmín la alfombra líquida
una lengua texturada un sofá de diez
cuerpos sobre el sofá otro cuerpo el olor
recorriéndolo de pies a cabeza amarillo
una ropa obligatoria creí que era
modernismo brasilero pero no es una
pierna.

ALICIA PREZA

translation by Julia Leverone

Sacrilege

No one asked us who we were.
Nor could they tell us
how they were able to see our faces
when the shadows left us naked.
We remember only one name.
We're prisoners of a story
but they closed the book.
A chill runs through my bones.
We're watched, at times, by the eye of a pencil.
But no one recognizes us.
We survived,
the hurricane no longer trembles.
No one asked us
if we could stand such beauty.
The library is in mourning.
A sacrilege of ink pursues us.
We breathed,
after having loved our own deaths.
The last page is broken.
Now we live, wandering,
begging for an end.

Sacrilegio

Nadie nos preguntó quiénes éramos.
Ni supieron decirnos,
como se veían nuestros rostros
cuando la penumbra nos dejaba desnudos.
Solo recordamos un nombre.
Somos prisioneros de una historia.
Cerraron el libro.
Un escalofrío recorre mis huesos.
A veces nos vigila el ojo de un lápiz.
Nadie nos reconoce.
Sobrevivimos,
ya no tiembla el huracán.
La biblioteca está de luto.
Un sacrilegio de tinta nos persigue.
Nadie nos preguntó
si podíamos soportar tanta belleza.
Respiramos,
luego de haber amado nuestra muerte.
Se quebró la última hoja.
Ahora vivimos, errantes,
suplicando un final.

Déjà Vu

I stare at the flower painted near the lip
but still she doesn't appear
I sit at night in the grass
the vessel in my hands
I remember her skirt
red bird shaking off shadow
monologue of light in my retina
days pass and nothing happens
I wait at the same hour
this spell will work that woman can't lie
there was a viper on her neck
a bit of venom in the ritual.
A whip sounds
I scratch at the vessel I reach its bottom
I feel warmth in my sex
I return to my room
there's a pool of lava
it must be her beneath my body.

Deja vú

Miro esa flor pintada en el extremo
pero ella no aparece todavía
me siento por las noches en el pasto
con la vasija entre mis manos
recuerdo su pollera
pájaro rojo sacudiendo la sombra
monólogo de luz en mi retina
pasan los días y nada sucede
sigo esperando a la misma hora
el conjuro funcionará esa mujer no miente
tenía una víbora en el cuello
un poco de veneno en el ritual.
Escucho ruido a látigo en el aire
araño la vasija hasta el fondo
siento algo tibio en mi sexo
regreso a mi habitación
hay un charco de lava
debe ser ella debajo de mi cuerpo.

The Spell

Long ago, I left my home.
In this new place, remote,
no one can find me.
An ancient woman took me in—
her age breeds gleeful bats.
The woman prepares a treat,
shuts herself in the kitchen.
Her dogs lie curled at my feet, waiting.
The aroma invades us.
I glance outside and am startled.
The rain is chocolate,
chocolate trees melt in the yard.
My sadness is chocolate, your chocolate eyes
set me shivering, I remember you.
Distant applause reaches us.
The woman opens the door
to offer the steaming dish.
She catches herself in the mirror and goes mad.
Her face is chocolate,
all her being sweet and pained.
The dogs approach, are hungry.
I want to save her but there's no time,
my breasts are leaking chocolate.
I can't help myself—
it hurts, eating myself,
it frightens me.
She yells, cries, prays.
The spell slowly lifts.
Our bodies become once again genuine,
can no longer be eaten.
The town is alert,
they look for explanations, investigate.

They are terrified of chocolate.
It was an accident, a moment of excess,
gruesome magic play.
I can no longer hide it.
I declare myself the culprit.

El hechizo

Hace tiempo que dejé mi casa,
en este lugar remoto
nadie puede encontrarme.
Me alberga una mujer antigua,
su vejez engendra murciélagos felices.
La mujer prepara un manjar,
se encerró en la cocina.
Sus perros esperan acurrucados a mis pies.
El aroma nos invade.
Miro hacia afuera y me asusto.
La lluvia es chocolate,
árboles de chocolate se derriten en el patio.
La tristeza es chocolate, tus ojos chocolate
me estremecen, te recuerdo.
Se oyen aplausos lejanos.
La mujer abre la puerta,
ofrece el manjar hirviente.
Se mira al espejo y enloquece.
Su rostro es chocolate,
todo su ser es dulce y doloroso.
Los perros se acercan, tienen hambre.
Quiero salvarla pero no hay tiempo,
mis senos gotean chocolate.
No puedo detenerme,
me duele comerme a mí misma,
me espanta.
La mujer grita, llora, reza.
El hechizo se desvanece lentamente.
Los cuerpos vuelven a ser genuinos,
ya nadie puede comernos.
El pueblo está alerta,
buscan explicaciones, investigan.

Tienen pánico al chocolate.
Fue un descuido, un exceso,
una terrible travesura de magia.
Ya no puedo ocultarlo,
me declaro culpable.

Olivetti

Thrown from the sixth floor. Clavicle of the poet, wary before the inert beast, spent after so much coughing up of unusable letters. The print of a finger left a heresy of dust on the keys. That unbearable sound always drilling at her mouth. "Your hidden part obsesses me." Your part is . . . She refused to say the rest, didn't finish the novel. Did she leave you hanging? The sweet little dessert of the night was melting, bitch of a word. She fed hundreds of pages into its skeleton until she heard the scream. Then she freed herself. Ungrateful bourgeoisie, you never had to steal bar napkins or work with the tip of an old pencil. The typewriter, I wanted her, I dreamed about her from below when I saw you screwing with her on the balcony. Now, seeing her dead, I try to reassemble her . . . she doesn't respond, sacred Olivetti, poor slave of what was written, I pray over your parts and curse the poet. Something survives in your departure, the drumming of that phrase you never gave to your assassin, your vengeance, Olivetti, is my delirium.

Olivetti

La tiró del sexto piso. Clavícula del poeta, desasosiego por la fiera inerte, rendida al fin de tanto escupir letras inservibles. La huella de un dedo dejó su herejía de polvo en las teclas. Ese ruido insoportable taladraba la boca. "Tu pieza hundida me obsesiona". Tu pieza es. . . Ella se negó a decir el resto, no cerró la novela, ¿te dejó con las ganas? Postrecito de noche se derrite, perra de la palabra. Le metió cientos de papeles en su esqueleto, uno por uno, hasta oírla gritar, después se libró de ella. Burgués ingrato, nunca tuviste que robar servilletas de los bares ni sacarle punta a un lápiz viejo a punto de quebrarse. Yo que siempre quise tener una, la soñé desde abajo cuando te veía copular con ella en el balcón. Y ahora, al verla muerta, intento armarla de nuevo pero no. . . ya no responde, sagrada Olivetti, cierva de lo escrito, rezo sobre tus partes y maldigo al poeta. Algo sobrevive en tu retiro, el aleteo de esa frase que no le diste al asesino, tu venganza, Olivetti, es mi delirio.

Scaffolding

for María Laura Blanco

Fearful pleasure kite
there goes the string/there it goes
the hand rises with it
escapes what it created
returns in another game
green paper fury
another necklace slips is no longer visible
lash of the offering
the dampened portrait doesn't show the laughter
the barb disarms, a shrine of sand
a lighthouse soliloquy in its bright river
the cords of your neck no one can touch them
you have something tattooed, it's not an object
your scaffolding collapses in the crying woman
one inside the other/Russian doll on the floor
there goes the string/there it goes
the hand releases the rapture of another body.

Entramado

a María Laura Blanco

Aterrada cometa del goce
se va el hilo/se va
la mano también sube
escapa lo creado
regresa en otro juego
papel verde la furia
otro collar resbala no es visible
látigo de la ofrenda
ese retrato húmedo no deja ver la risa
la púa se desarma, relicario de arena
soliloquio del faro en su río de luz
las hebras de tu cuello nadie puede tocarlas
llevas algo tatuado no es objeto
tu entramado se pierde en la mujer que llora
una dentro de la otra/muñeca rusa en el suelo
se va el hilo/se va
la mano suelta el rapto de otro cuerpo.

SEBASTIÁN RIVERO

translation by Catherine Jagoe

No Name

jails like
tunnels in blood

animals vanish
down tortuous paths
squeeze their bodies
into sewers

on beaches
unnamed body bags
sprawl slack in seaweed

the memory of your
childhood
that seaside light

you cannot see the
silver foxtails
in the forests

muscles rip
on the rack

what music
        modulates
the glare?

voices, words, echoes

trace the whirlwind's edge

*foxtails under the
moon
in the forests*

the scent of eucalyptus

beaches covered with
black bags

your blood squeezed
into the corridors
of arteries

in the furnaces

the national rituals

jail

exile

inxile

borders

but later

                    your blood

boiling

                    in revolt

I'm blind, I'm blind

give me a name

cover my eyes

shoot me, drown me
please give me

a name

at the end

        the tunnel

light

        at the end

just that

everyday crimes

bags on the beaches
of your childhood   *(can you see them?*
                                        do you remember?
                                        did they tell you?)

masking the scent

of eucalyptus   *(have you ever smelled it?)*

in the silver forests
of moonlight
and the wind wailing
among the foxtails

jail

a name

the nation   *(were you there? was I?*
                                   did anyone tell me?)

between the margins

                identity.

N. N.

cárceles como
túneles en la sangre

los animales se escurren
recorren los caminos tortuosos
adelgazan sus cuerpos
en las alcantarillas

en las playas se desploman
las bolsas con los N. N.
entre las algas

el recuerdo de tu
infancia
la luz sobre las playas

no puedes ver las
colas de zorro plateadas
en los bosques

revientan los músculos
bajo el torno

¿qué música
       modula
el resplandor?

voces, palabras, ecos

traza el límite del torbellino

*las colas de zorro bajo la
luna
en los bosques*

el olor a eucaliptos

las playas cubiertas de
bolsas negras

tu sangre apretada
en los corredores
en las arterias

en los altos hornos

los rituales de la patria

la cárcel

el exilio

el inxilio

las fronteras

pero luego

                      tu sangre

bullendo

                      en rebeldía

estoy ciego, estoy ciego

dame un nombre

cubre mis ojos

dispárame, ahógame

dame, por favor

un nombre

al final

        el túnel

la luz

        al final

tan simple

crímenes cotidianos

bolsas en las playas

de tu infancia   *(¿las ves?*
                                  ¿recuerdas?
                                  ¿te dijeron?)

cubriendo el olor

a eucaliptos   *(¿oliste alguna vez?)*

en los bosques plateados
por la luna
y el viento ululando
entre las colas de zorro

la cárcel

un nombre

la patria   *(¿estuvo?¿estuve?*
                         ¿acaso me dijeron?)

entre los márgenes

                    la identidad.

mud

they lived in huts
ate fish, hares, birds
frogs and butterflies
they hunted with spears, bows,
boleadoras, stones and spoons
one day they went west
and are now extinct.

(thanks to the law of eternal return they're back: in the plazas,
  on altars, in almanacs, in the laws, in the obituaries, white,
  black, yellow, green, and blue, with feathers or without, in
  commercials, in video clips, they come back . . . but they
  didn't ask to)

(May 5, 1607—from Hernandarias to his king)

"will spend the next year with some men and horses exploring
  the other shore, which is called the Charrúa coast (. . .). And
  if I find it suitable and well protected as I do imagine, and if
  it seems to me to behoove your Royal Service, it should be
  possible to establish a settlement there that I believe would be
  of importance to the said matter and of no less consequence
  for other reasons, and so as to hold criminals and those who
  come without order and license from Your Majesty, for once
  they set foot here there is no way to arrest them or at least
  they have ample chance of fleeing."

the river nearby
a hoarse roar
pressing down
bending the night
to its will
everything wanes here
collapses

        dies

in dense matter

fermented in the depths

modernity never makes it here

mud
        splashing mud

someone on the ships said:

something knots, sticks
in the throat
chewed
with patriotic zeal
a ration of disinfected
poultices
chewing, ruminating
our thinning flesh
sticking to our ribs
the bastard daughters
of famine

footsteps trailing mud

        licking the coasts

city of mud

unconscious life

        in the waves' undertow

drawing circles

(tuneless cries of seagulls)

where, out of nothing, the city is founded

excessive hunger is a dire calamity

        hunger the cruelest malady

writes poet-chronicler Martín del Barco Centenera ruefully

(but when this tyrant

tempted brother with dead brother

        his lungs and entrails

        he did eat

        moste joyfullye).

(July 2, 1608—from Hernandarias to his king)

"and I traveled inland seeing the whole country (. . .) everything grows with great abundance and fertility and it is good for all kinds of livestock (. . .) ample amounts of hides and other fruits of the earth that grow in great abundance."

(leather, chewed and stretched leather, covering the animals and plants, because everything comes down to skin here, to dry, rotting death . . . we will sell our own skins, we will be quivering flesh, grieving soul, exposed).

barro

vivían en chozas
comían pescados, liebres, pájaros
ranas y mariposas
cazaban con lanzas, arcos,
boleadoras, piedras y cucharas
un día marcharon al poniente
ya se extinguieron.

(por la ley del eterno retorno vuelven: en las plazas, altares, almanaques, en las leyes, en los obituarios, blancos, negros, amarillos, verdes y azules, con plumas o sin plumas, en las tandas comerciales, en los videoclips, vuelven. . . pero ellos no lo pidieron)

(5 de mayo de 1607 —de Hernandarias a su rey)

"pasar este año que viene con alguna gente y caballos y correr la otra banda que llaman de los charrúas (. . .). Y si lo hallare dispuesto y fuerte de la suerte que yo imagino, y me pareciere convenir a vuestro Real Servicio será posible dejar poblado allí un pueblo que entiendo sería de importancia para lo dicho y de no menos efecto para otras ocasiones, y para tener allí los delincuentes y los que vienen sin orden y licencia de Vuestra Majestad porque poniendo los pies aquí no hay remedio para detenerlos o a lo menos tienen mucho para huirse".

el río alrededor
un ronco bramido
presionando
amoldando la noche
a sus caprichos
aquí se apaga todo
cae

        se muere

en materia densa

cocida en el fondo

aquí la modernidad nunca llega

barro

        chapoteando barro

alguien desde los barcos dijo:

algo se ata, se atora
en la garganta
masticado
con unción patria
ración de ungüentos
desinfectados
masticando, rumiando
la propia carne escasa
prendida a las ijadas
hijas ilegítimas
del hambre

pisadas arrastrando barro

        lamiendo las costas

ciudad de barro

vida inconsciente

        en la resaca que traen las olas

dibujar círculos

(graznidos afónicos de gaviotas)

donde, entre nada, se funda la ciudad

es grave mal la hambre en demasía

        hambre la enfermedad la más rabiosa

afirmó (con pudor)
el poeta-cronista Martín del Barco Centenera

(pero cuando tienta este tirano

un hermano al otro muerto

        bofes y asaduras

        le masca

        muy gozoso)

(2 de julio de 1608 —de Hernandarias a su rey)

"y volví por la tierra adentro viéndola toda (...) se da todo con grande abundancia y fertilidad y buena para todo género de ganados (...) gran suma de corambre y otros frutos de la tierra que se darán en grande abundancia".

(cuero, mascado y estirado cuero, revistiendo a los animales y plantas, porque todo se reduce al pellejo aquí, a la muerte seca y putrefacta... venderemos nuestro propio cuero, seremos carne vibrante, alma doliente, al desnudo.)

JUAN MANUEL SÁNCHEZ
translation by Cindy Schuster

from *For the Seals*

I.
Of late
the city
is awash
with seals.

Seals at my heels
penguinized seals
chimney-smoking
seals in meetings.

Seals
sealing deals
drinking scotch
on the rocks.

I lock myself
in the bathroom
I need
legs.

I too
applaud
and balance
a ball
on my nose.

XI.
I am going to pray
at the bank
where God
will hear my pleas.

Give us this day
our daily
clients.

There is no salvation
without work
nor work without profits.

Collect our debts
as we too
collect
from our debtors.

And deliver us
from recession
amen.

XII.
The boss is my shepherd
he leads me through
fertile valleys
of perpetual bonanza
spacious offices
and exclusive perks.

That is why I wait
for the next life
each day
is one day
closer
to the next life.

The boss is my shepherd
I shall not fear
when we traverse
dark paths.
And when he asks
for a test of my faith
I will flagellate my wages
and tighten the cilice
of my rights.

XIII.
Money
doesn't smell
and the higher
the figure
the fainter the scent.

No matter
if it springs
from the sweat
of my brow
or the blood
of others.

Money
doesn't smell
but as a precaution
only as a precaution
I always buy
the most expensive
perfume.

de *Para las focas*

I.
Últimamente
la ciudad
se ha llenado
de focas.

Focas en la sopa
focas apingüinadas
meeting de focas
fumando
chimeneas.

Focas
focas en la rocas
tomando
un buen scotch.

Me encierro
en el baño
necesito
piernas.

Yo también
aplaudo
y sostengo
la pelota
con mi hocico.

XI.
Voy a orar
al banco
donde Dios
oirá mis plegarias.

Danos hoy
nuestros clientes
de cada día.

No hay
salvación sin trabajo
ni trabajo sin ganancias.

Cobra nuestras deudas
como también
nosotros
cobramos
a quienes nos
adeudan.

Y líbranos
de la recesión
amén.

XII.
El gerente es mi pastor
me conduce por
fértiles valles
de bonanza perpetua
amplias oficinas
y exclusivos privilegios.

Por eso aguardo
la próxima vida
cada día
es un día
más cerca
de la próxima vida.

El gerente es mi pastor
no tendré miedo
cuando atravesemos
senderos oscuros.
Y cuando me pida
probar mi fe
flagelaré mi sueldo
y apretaré el cilicio
de mis derechos.

XIII.
El dinero
no tiene olor
y cuanto más cifras
tiene
menos huele.

Poco da
si brota
del sudor
de mi frente
o la sangre
de los otros.

El dinero
no tiene olor
pero por las dudas
sólo por las dudas
compro siempre
el perfume
más caro.

Untitled

Across a sea of grassland they came
people of curved sabers
olive skin and sacred stallions.

Agents of chaos, sons of destruction
weddings of the dead and revelry.

Cement
municipal decrees
arrogant tinted glass
containment plans
in civic centers,
all were futile.

Amid red-tinged clouds of smoke
rises
the city that never should have been.

Sin título

Llegaron a través de un mar de pasturas
pueblo de espadas curvas,
tez oliva y sementales sagrados.

Agentes del caos, hijos de la destrucción
bodas de muertos y en fiesta.

De nada sirvió el cemento
los decretos municipales
el arrogante vidrio polarizado
los planes de contención
por centros comunales.

En rojizas humaredas
se eleva
la ciudad que nunca debió existir.

FABIÁN SEVERO

translation by Dan Bellm

from *Night Up North*

Two.
Artigas is an abandoned station
the hope left behind by a train that won't come back
a road that disappears heading south.

Three.
I don't know how it is in civilized places
but in Artigas
people have a last name.
Mr. Nobodies
like me—
we come from the border.
Not from this side, not from the other.
The ground we walk on isn't ours
nor the language we speak.

Nine.
Artigas has a language that nobody owns.

Ten.
This tongue of mine
sticks out its tongue at the dictionary
dances a *pagode*[1] on top of the map
makes a kite from a schoolboy's tunic and sash
flies loose and free in the sky.

Eleven.
Artigas is a land lost up North
that doesn't show up on maps.

---

1. *Pagode* is a samba dance form.

Twelve.
Artigas had a sky filled with stars
a river of fish
fields green with trees
earth brilliant with stones
but someone's taken it all some other place
and we're left with nothing.

Thirteen.
Before
I wanted to be from Uruguay.
Now
I want to be from here.

Seventeen.
I don't go where the buses go—
I'm afraid I wouldn't find there
the things that I like.
In Artigas in the morning
I see lamps lit in doorways with nylon curtains
hunkered-down dogs keeping watch
house numbers whitewashed on unplastered walls
yards full of weeds
washtubs leaning on wires for hanging out clothes
windows with flowerpots in bloom
houses half-built
and always open.

Eighteen.
The hour when the sun becomes hidden—
that's the time when you listen.
The stars press out and light up the fireflies.
The crickets sing
that bring good luck.
I close the front door

and go into myself so I can think,
so I'm able to write.

Nineteen.
The Río Cuareim flows out back;
sometimes it sings, sometimes it sleeps.
It flows downhill and goes
and goes who knows where.
The fishes are free; I think they go with the river,
just go to wherever it ends—
they say that's the sea,
a place where the water doesn't touch the earth.

Twenty-three.
I didn't know what I could write
until my godfather said one day,
Yiribibe, tu vas fasé istoria:
You'll make up stories, kid.
He didn't use those words.
He spoke very well.
So I started to write.
I enjoy the nights up North.
The flies are asleep
and I write in the notebook *la Negra* gave me.

My *padrino* was right,
I wasn't going to end up like Mónica's kids,
good for nothing but gossip and scandal.
I hooked up with *la Negra*,
then I found work at Arrieta's place.
Now we have a house, and we're expecting a child.

I write to show the boy when he starts asking questions.
La Negra's nephew must be about five years old—
I see him always asking.

Children these days are a guiding light.
They want to know everything, and they never stop.

Thirty-four.
My mother spoke perfectly well, and I understood.
Fabi anda faser los deber, and I'd do my chores.
Fabi traseme meio litro de leite, I brought her half a liter of milk.
Desí pra doña Cora que amañá le pago—
I told Doña Cora she'd get paid tomorrow.
Deya iso gurí—stop that, child—and I would stop.

But my teacher didn't understand.
She'd send home letters in my notebook
all in red, like her face, and signed at the bottom.

But my mother didn't understand.
Le iso pra mim, ijo, and I'd read them to her.

But my mother didn't understand.
Que fiseste meu fío—what did you do, child—
te dise que portaras bien, and I *did* behave myself.

The story repeated itself for months.
My teacher wrote, but my mother didn't understand.
My teacher wrote, but my mother didn't understand.

Then one day my mother understood.
She said, *Meu fío, tu terás que deiyá la iscuela*—
so I quit that school.

Forty.
When I'd go to my *padrino*'s house
I'd see my *madrina* giving a bath to Luisa
who had blond hair and blue eyes
and she'd say

Viste Yiribibe—watch me, boy.
If you want to turn out like Luisa,
you've got to scrub hard, and the water has to be hot.

So I spent hours washing
got red in the face from scrubbing myself so much
burned myself with hot water
but I kept on being black.

Forty-one.
Fito would always say, *God helps the early risers.*
And God always helped him.
I'd try to get up before he did
but he was always first, and God helped *him*.

Whenever I woke up
I'd look outside and see him sitting there,
hunched over, skinny,
drinking sweet *mate* and eating bread
left over from yesterday.

That's how it was in our house.
God helped the one who got up first.
Those of us who didn't
had to wait until noon
for something to eat.

Fifty-eight.
We come from the border
like the sun that's born here
behind the eucalyptus trees
and shines on everything over the river
then goes off to sleep
behind the Rodríguezes' house.

From the border
just like the moon
that turns night almost to day
laying down its light
on the banks of the Cuareim.

Like the wind
that makes the flags dance
when the rain
carries off the houses on the other side
right along with ours.

We all come from the border
when birds fly in from over there
singing in a language
we all understand.

We came from the border
we head to the border
when grandparents and children
eat the godforsaken bread
of affliction
at this end of the earth.

We are the border
more than any river
more than any bridge.

de *Noite nu norte / Noche en el norte*

Dois.
Artigas e uma estasión abandonada
a esperansa ditrás de um trein que no regresa
uma ruta que se perde rumbo ao sur.

Treis.
Noum sei como será nas terra sivilisada
mas ein Artigas
viven los que tienen apeyido.
Los Se Ninguéim
como eu
semo da frontera
neim daquí neim dalí
no es noso u suelo que pisamo
neim a lingua que falemo.

Nove.
Artigas teim uma lingua sin dueño.

Des.
Miña lingua le saca la lengua al disionario
baila um pagode ensima dus mapa
i fas com a túnica i a moña uma cometa
pra voar, livre i solta pelu seu.

Onse.
Artigas e uma terra pirdida nu Norte
qui noum sai nus mapa.

Dose.
Artigas tevi um seu yeio distrela
um río yeio de peiye
um campo verde, asím de árbol

uma terra briliante de pedra
mas alguém levou tudo pra otru povo
i nos fiquemo seim nada.

Tresi.
Antes,
eu quiría ser uruguaio
agora
quiero ser daquí.

Disesete.
Yo no voi pra donde van los ónibus
pois teño medo de no incontrar las cosa que gosto.
En Artigas, por las mañá
veyo lamparitas asesas
nas puerta con cortina de nailon
i us cayorro deitado, viyilando.
Números pintado con cal nas parede sin revocar
patios yeio de yuyo disparejo
as pileta arrecostada nus alambre pra tender ropa
yanelas con maseta rompida
casas pur a metade
i siempre abertas.

Chisoito.
Na ora qui u sol sisconde es la ora qui um iscuta.
Las estreya impurran i asenden los biyo de lus.
Cantan los griyo que trasen boa suerte.
Eu feyo la portera
i me adentro em mim pra matutar
i pudé iscrevé.

Disenove.
El río Cuareim camiña nus fundo
asvés canta, asvés dorme.

Camiña pra abayo, i se vai, se vai asta noum sei onde.
Los peye som livre i yo ayo que se van con el río
se van pra onde ele termiña
dis que es nu mar
um lugar aonde la agua noum toca la tierra.

Vintitrés.
Yo no sabía que pudía iscrevé
asta que mi padriño un día dise
Yiribibe, tu vas fasé istoria.
El no dise con esas palavra
purque el falava mui bien.
Intonse impesé iscrevé.
Aproveito las noite nu Norte
nou avoa uma mosca i iscrevo nu caderno
presente de la Negra.

Meu padriño tava serto
yo no ía terminar como us fío da Mónica
aqueles nou presta pra nada, so pra fofoca.
Eu me yuntei con la Negra
dispós consiguí imprego nus Arrieta
agora temo casa i tamo isperando ijo.

Yo iscrevo pra amostrar el día que u gurí pergunte.
Yo veyo quel subriño da Negra
que deve andar pelos sinco ano, pergunta tudo.
Los gurí de agora son una lus
quereim sabé tudo i noum se calam nunca.

Trinticuatro.
Mi madre falava mui bien, yo intendía.
Fabi andá faser los deber, yo fasía.
Fabi traseme meio litro de leite, yo trasía.
Desí pra doña Cora que amañá le pago, yo disía.

Deya iso gurí, i yo deiyava.

Mas mi maestra no intendía.
Mandava cartas en mi caderno
todo con rojo (igualsito su cara) i asinava imbaiyo.

Mas mi madre no intendía.
Le iso pra mim, ijo, i yo leía.

Mas mi madre no intendía.
Qué fiseste meu fío, te dise que te portaras bien
i yo me portava.

A istoria se repitió por muintos mes.
Mi maestra iscrevía, mas mi madre no intendía.
Mi maestra iscrevía, mas mi madre no intendía.

Intonses serto día mi madre intendió i dise:
Meu fío, tu terás que deiyá la iscuela
i yo deiyé.

Cuarenta.
Cuando yo iva na casa de mi padriño
vía como mi madriña bañava la Luisa
que era ruiva i oios claro
i ela disía
Viste Yiribibe, para que fiques igual que la Luisa
tenés que fregarte bein forte i con agua bein caliente.
Yo pasava oras me lavando
ficava colorado de tanto misfregar
i me queimava con la agua quente
mas siguía siendo negro.

Cuarentaiúm.
El Fito sempre disía, *quien madruga Dios lo ayuda.*
I Dios sempre le ayudava.

Yo tentava me levantá antes quel
mas ele sempre gañava y Deus ayudava ele.
Cuando yo me despertava
oiava pra la i lo veía sentado
jorovado i magro
tomando mate dose i cumendo el pan
que avía sobrado de onteim.

Nas casa era asím
el que se levantava primero, Deus le ayudava.
Us que noum madrugava
tíñamos que isperar asta u meiodía
pra pudé cumé.

Sincuentioito.
Nos semo da frontera
como u sol qui nase alí tras us ucalito
alumeia todo u día ensima du río
i vai durmí la despós da casa dus Rodrígues.

Da frontera como a lua
qui fas a noite cuasi día
deitando luar nas maryen del Cuareim.

Como el viento
que ase bailar las bandera
como a yuva
leva us ranyo deles yunto con los nuestro.

Todos nos semo da frontera
como eses pásaro avuando de la pra qui
cantando um idioma que todos intende.

Viemos da frontera
vamo pra frontera

como us avó i nosos filio
cumendo el pan que u diabo amasó
sofrendo neste fin de mundo.

Nos semo a frontera
mas que cualqué río
mas que cualqué puente.

PAULA SIMONETTI

translation by Catherine Jagoe

Isabel

There's an autumn caught in her name
her husband and her sight are gone
now she lives with other derelicts
she sees nothing
no one sees her
the faces of grief moving shadows
the plate of food wobbles
I don't want to watch it fall
again and again
you don't see / the cold or the poem
you don't know the shape of my face
you carry that dead man on your bent back
lie sleepless listening to others sleep
that room / the sound of lungs the wheezing
music of indigence in that room
"no one will come Isabel because there is no one" you murmur
smoking without seeing the courtyard
there's an autumn caught in my eyes
no one will come Isabel because there is no one

Isabel

Hay un otoño que se le quedó en el nombre
el marido que no está y esa ceguera
ahora vive con otros miserables
no mira nada
nadie la mira
los rostros de la pena sombras móviles
el plato de comida tambalea
ya ni quiero ver cómo se cae
una y otra vez
no ves / el frío ni el poema
no sabés la forma de mi cara
cargás al hombre muerto sobre la joroba
y escuchás despierta el sueño de los compañeros
esa pieza / el ruido de pulmones los silbidos
la música de la miseria en esa pieza
—nadie vendrá Isabel porque no hay nadie —murmurás
fumando sin poder mirar el patio
hay un otoño que se me quedó en los ojos
nadie vendrá Isabel porque no hay nadie

Nelson

He plays with the rice on his plate, making shapes
I pray for you, always so quiet
you who never complain
in the cigarette ash you look
for the shapes of love / or your children
hours in wintertime when you raise worlds of ash
stains on the ceiling where the eye traces a dog
a woman
the faces you've loved the most
a lamp in the night / returning and it's
almost dawn
you dream of the shapes in the rice / the ash
you reinvent your wife / you gaze
at the dog as night falls and in sleep you wait
for the faces of your children to prolong your dream

Nelson

Revuelve el arroz para armar figuras en el plato
pido por vos que sabés guardar silencio y no quejarte
buscás en las cenizas del tabaco
las formas del amor / las de tus hijos
horas de invierno en que levantás los mundos de ceniza
manchas en el techo donde el ojo va trazando al perro
a la mujer
los rostros más queridos
una lámpara en la noche / ese regreso y es
de madrugada
soñás con las formas del arroz / de la ceniza
volvés a inventar a tu mujer / mirás
al perro cuando cae la noche y esperás dormido
las caras de los hijos donde prolongar tu sueño

Gisela

They don't wait for visitors in winter
or wave a welcome
they contemplate their plates
wash clothes
They long for summer and at night
amid the soup-time chaos and the yelling
there goes the little girl
please
may your mother's screams not touch you
the words that grown-ups say to one another
nothing
Teacher I raise my hand too
though I no longer believe in anything please
may the wheeze not touch your lungs
the cigarette smoke the faucets
may you not hear the sound of that slap
may your mother's breath not touch you
may the air not touch you nor the poem

Gisela

No esperan visitas en invierno
ni agitan las manos en señal de bienvenida
miran el plato
lavan la ropa
Piden el verano y a la noche
entre el desorden de la sopa y de los gritos
pasa la niña
pido
que no te toquen los gritos de tu madre
las palabras que se dicen los adultos
nada
Maestro yo también alzo los brazos
aunque ya no creo en nada pido
que no te toquen los pulmones los silbidos
el humo de tabaco las canillas
que no sientas ni el ruido de esa cachetada
que no te toque el aliento de tu madre
que no te toque el aire ni el poema

Ramón

The man who paints points to the wall
tells me about hunger and the exiles
the man who paints shivers in colors
he spews out his life when he coughs / spits blood
Vallejo is everywhere
squalor is red when it hits the wall
when they cough it up
it peers out of the chest / spits and survives
the man talks about evictions, hardships
he opens a hole in words
our father in the prayer the man is painting
he whispers in the night
embraces night
and in the night paints this poem

Ramón

El hombre que pinta señala la pared
me cuenta sobre el hambre y los exilios
el hombre que pinta tiembla en los colores
arroja la vida cuando tose / escupe sangre
y es Vallejo que está por todas partes
la miseria es roja cuando estalla en la pared
cuando la tosen
se asoma al pecho / escupe y sobrevive
el hombre cuenta desalojos o miserias
abre un agujero en las palabras
padre nuestro en la oración que el hombre pinta
susurra en la noche
a la noche abraza
y en la noche va pintando este poema

What the Sad Say

I could be the breath of fresh
the last sigh or the shape
of all the objects in this house
Miguel dreamed he was stealing a thermos flask
a cup a shirt
the world itself
and other things that aren't as sad
thirst has such a deep face
it's a hole a well that keeps on growing
while the heart keeps beating
Isabel keeps looking for a tiny
territory in her bed
where she can fall apart and no one will notice
I could be the wrong line
wear loneliness like
a pebble in the pocket or else
I could be the tea the sick sip
I could be the mouth of the sick man
the bird that flits and won't alight
I could be the broom sweeping sleep away
or my own hands resisting
the interminable well of thirst
but I am the earth or a name
people say when they're hungry
I'm the invisible hand that brings you
one or two thermometers a day
I
am the same hand that holds
Isabel's plate or the heart
that's just dropped
I'm a woman who opens the door
for Nelson to take out the trash
I'm the voice announcing lunch
a shadow they go looking for
just a name the sad say

En la boca de los tristes

Yo podría ser la bocanada
el último suspiro o ser la forma
de todos los objetos de esta casa
Miguel soñó que se robaba un termo
una taza una camisa
soñó que se robaba el mundo
y otras cosas menos tristes
la sed tiene un rostro tan profundo
es un hueco un pozo que se ensancha
a medida que suceden los latidos
Isabel sigue buscando un territorio
ínfimo adentro de su cama
donde romperse sin que nadie diga nada
yo podría ser el trazo confundido
llevar la soledad como se lleva
una piedra en el bolsillo o ser
el té que se beben los enfermos
yo podría ser la boca del enfermo
el pájaro fugaz que no se posa
ser la escoba con que se retira el sueño
o ser mis propias manos resistiendo
el pozo interminable de la sed
pero soy la tierra o soy un nombre
que dicen las personas cuando tienen hambre
soy la mano invisible que te acerca
uno o dos termómetros por día
soy
la misma mano que sostiene
el plato de Isabel o el corazón
que de repente se me cae
soy una mujer que abre la puerta
para que Nelson tire la basura
soy la voz que anuncia la comida
una sombra que buscan por la casa
solo un nombre en la boca de los tristes

KAREN WILD DÍAZ

translation by Ron Paul Salutsky

Thread of Blood in the Sky

In the sky a thread of blood
Like a stream on a map,
like a stream of a continent on a map

The map is in the sky
and we bend back our necks to see

The map is in the sky
and is unreachable as the map
The map seems reachable
but is not enough to be tangible to be
The map, nonetheless, is
but so unreachable

So the sky has a thread

Wants not to fall from nothing. Wants to live
Wants not to fall nonetheless. There is no

Certainty it will appear
They say the sky will not fall on our head
Will not fall is what they say

When the threads fall in torment,
how surely they fall and torment,
we must remain standing

When the blood falls on us

Wanting, wanting. To make something of the blood
but something that is not anything
Wanting, wanting. Remain standing
Neck back. When the thread of blood

Falls,
when in torment soaks us,
our desire shall become
An act. An unspecified act
In principle, it can be anything
but is not just anything. Something must be done

The sky has a thread
Look
You shall not hope for anything
to happen. Nothing

No desire to fall: it's in your blood
Do not

Hilo de sangre en el cielo

Hay un hilo de sangre en el cielo
Como un arroyo en un mapa,
como un arroyo de un continente en un mapa

El mapa está en el cielo
y nosotros doblamos la nuca hacia atrás para ver

El mapa está en el cielo
y es inalcanzable como el mapa
El mapa parece alcanzable
pero no es suficiente ser tangible para ser
El mapa, sin embargo, es
pero de modo inalcanzable

Por eso, el cielo tiene un hilo

No quiere caerse desde nada. Quiere vivir
No quiere caerse sin embargo. No lo hará

Hay certezas parece
Dicen que el cielo no nos caerá en la cabeza
Que no caerá es lo que dicen

Cuando se atormente y caiga en hilos,
seguro se atormenta y caen,
hay que estarse en pie

Cuando nos caigan con sangre

Querer, querer. Hacer algo con la sangre
Pero algo que no es cualquier cosa
Querer, querer. Estarse en pie
Nuca hacia atrás. El hilo de sangre

Cuando caiga,
cuando atormente y nos moje,
habrá que hacer algo
Querer algo. Hacer algo
Que no es cualquier cosa
En principio, cualquier cosa puede ser
Pero no es cualquier cosa. Hay que hacer algo

El cielo tiene un hilo
Mira
No esperes que pase
Algo. Nada

No quiere caerse: está en su sangre
No lo hará

Shelter from the Sky

She protects her head from the sky

The sky is a place way up

She rises endlessly to the sky
Walk or climb the sky is endless
She suffers because the sky is a place
she cannot reach and she rises
Stops, and leans down

The sky is a place below

She furrows her brow
and pushes through a snag
to rise

The path to the sky falls away in a bend
seems a surefooted place
the sky is nowhere

The sky is no place at all

Protege del cielo

Ella protege su cabeza del cielo

El cielo es un lugar muy alto

Ella no para de subir al cielo
Camine o trepe el cielo es un lugar que no para
Ella sufre porque el cielo es un lugar
que no se alcanza y sube
Detiene, se apoya y que baje

El cielo es un lugar que baja

Ella frunce el ceño
y le pega un empujón
para que suba

Camino al cielo se desploma en un recodo
siente como un lugar muy cierto
que el cielo no es en parte alguna

El cielo no es ningún lugar

The Sky Knows No Walls

If it is very cold
and you're out in the open
Find a wall to lean on

A wall is something very tall
After a wall another wall
that grows
Then continues on the wall
and adds more walls
Up to the sky
The sky knows no walls
She lifts her face to the sky
and leans on the walls

Always fantasizes crossing the wall
and finding on the other side
        the sky
        the water

El cielo no conoce las paredes

Si hace mucho frío
y estás en un lugar abierto
Procura apoyarte en una pared

Una pared es una cosa muy alta
Después de una pared hay otra pared
que crece
Después se continúa en la pared
y se suman más paredes
Hasta el cielo
El cielo no conoce las paredes
Ella sube cara al cielo
Se apoya en las paredes

Siempre fantasea que atraviesa la pared
y encuentra al otro lado
        el cielo
        el agua

A House without the Sky

She can live in a house without the sky
Light a candle, walk on all fours

Do not wash your hands upon entering
Before writing do not wash your hands
You will lose the essence
She does not believe in essences
Does not wash her hands and she writes

She can live in a house without the sky but
cannot stand to be indoors for long
The longing lives always in her
and beyond

She covers her head
The sky is a place way up
and outside of her longing is involved
with this hand that does not wash
and wicks away inside her dark house
where she lights a candle
to open the faucet and run the water

She troubles herself with the roof and leaves
She tires of being outside and seeks

A home where she could sit down at the table

Una casa sin cielo

Ella puede vivir en una casa sin cielo
Prende una vela, camina a gatas

No te laves las manos cuando entres
Antes de escribir no te laves las manos
Perderás la esencia
Ella no cree en las esencias
No se lava las manos y escribe

Ella puede vivir en una casa sin cielo pero
no soporta estar adentro mucho rato
Su anhelo habita siempre en ella
y más allá

Ella protege su cabeza
El cielo es un lugar muy alto
y el afuera de su anhelo está implicado
en esta mano que no lava
y lleva por adentro de su casa oscura
donde prende una vela
para abrir el grifo y corra el agua

Ella se molesta por el techo y sale
Ella se cansa del afuera y busca

Una casa donde pueda sentarse a la mesa

Contributors

Poets

MIGUEL AVERO was born in Montevideo, Uruguay, in 1984. He is studying at the Instituto de Profesores Artigas to be a literature teacher. He is a founder of Orientación Poesía, which brings poetry readings and workshops to high schools throughout Uruguay. He is the author of the poetry collection *Arca de aserrín* and the story collection *Micaela Moon*. His poems have appeared in the *Beltway Poetry Quarterly*, *Rio Grande Review*, *Palabras Errantes: Latin American Literature in Translation*, and *Prairie Schooner*. The Uruguayan poets who have influenced him are Líber Falco, Saúl Pérez Gadea, and Leonardo de León; the American poets, Paul Auster and Charles Bukowski.

MARTÍN BAREA MATTOS was born in Montevideo in 1978. He is a visual artist, a musician, and the author of the poetry collections *Conexo*, *Por hora por día por mes*, *Los ojos escritos*, *Dos mil novecientos noventa y cinco*, and *Fuga de ida y vuelta*. His collection *Never Made in America: Selected Poems in Translation*, translated by Mark Statman, will be published in the United States by Lavender Ink in 2017. He is the organizer of the long-running Montevideo reading series Ronda de Poetas. The poets who most influenced him are the Uruguayan Juvenal Ortiz Saralegui; Federico García Lorca of Spain; and the American Jack Kerouac.

HORACIO CAVALLO was born in Montevideo in 1977. He is the author of twelve books, including the poetry collections *El revés asombrado de la ocarina*, *Descendencia*, and *Sonetos a dos*, coauthored with Francisco Tomsich. He has participated in literary festivals in Mexico, Brazil, Venezuela, Chile, and Bolivia. Poems from *Sonetos a dos* have appeared in *Palabras Errantes*. He admires the Uruguayan poets Washington Benavides, Jorge Meretta, Álvaro Figueredo, and Alfredo Fressia and the English-language poets William Shakespeare and Raymond Carver.

MARTÍN CERISOLA was born in Porto Alegre, Brazil, in 1979. He is a poet, performer, essayist, and teacher. He is the author of the book of essays *Orfismo y errancia* and the poetry collection *Perseguir*. His poems have appeared in *Palabras Errantes*. His favorite Uruguayan poets are Idea Vilariño and Cecilio Peña. He admires the work of Sylvia Plath and is also influenced by Hugo Mujica, Antonio Gamoneda, San Juan de la Cruz, Rainer Maria Rilke, and Paul Celan.

LAURA CESARCO EGLIN was born in Montevideo in 1976. She is the author of three poetry collections, *Llamar al agua por su nombre*, *Sastrería*, and *Los brazos del saguaro*. Her poems have appeared in *Copper Nickel* and *Palabras Errantes*. She holds a master's degree in English from the Hebrew University of Jerusalem, earned an MFA in creative writing from the University of Texas at El Paso, and is currently a doctoral candidate at the University of Colorado Boulder. Among the Uruguayan poets she admires are Idea Vilariño, Marosa di Giorgio, and Ida Vitale. Her other influences include Alejandra Pizarnik and César Vallejo.

LAURA CHALAR was born in Montevideo in 1976. She is a lawyer, poet, and translator. Her books include the story collections *El discreto encanto de la abogacía* and *El vuelo del pterodáctilo* and the poetry collections *por así decirlo* and *Por qué los poetas ingleses quieren morir en Italia*. Her poems have appeared in *Palabras Errantes*, *Interim*, and the *Notre Dame Review*. Her work is influenced by the Uruguayan poets Líber Falco and Marosa di Giorgio; the Americans Walt Whitman, Adrienne Rich, and Emily Dickinson; and the Montevideo-born French poet Jules Supervielle.

ANDREA DURLACHER was born in Montevideo in 1984. She writes columns for the Uruguayan newspapers *El País* and *El Observador* and conducts private creative writing workshops. She published the novel *Esto es una pipa* and the poetry collection *Ni un segundo para arrepentirme*. Her poems have appeared in *Palabras Errantes* and *Words without Borders*. Among her favorite poets are the Uruguayan Julio Herrera y Reissig and the American Emily Dickinson. Her work is also influenced by César Vallejo and Fernando Pessoa.

VICTORIA ESTOL was born in Montevideo in 1983. She is a sociologist and a student of psychology. *Bicho Bola*, her book of poetry, translated by Seth Michelson, was published in English as *Roly Poly*. Her poems have appeared in the *Colorado Review*, *spoKe*, and *Words without Borders*. Her favorite poets include the Uruguayan Cristina Carneiro, the Argentine Oliverio Girondo, and the American Raymond Carver.

JAVIER ETCHEVARREN was born in Montevideo in 1979. His two poetry collections are *Desidia* and *Fábula de un hombre desconsolado*. His poems have been published in *ME USA*, a Peruvian anthology, and the *American Literary Review*, *Blue Lyra Review*, *Notre Dame Review*, *Palabras Errantes*, and *Waxwing*. The Uruguayan poet who influenced him most is Jorge Meretta. He admires the American poets Allen Ginsberg and Charles Bukowski.

PAOLA GALLO was born in Montevideo in 1980. She holds a master's degree in modern letters from the Universidad Iberoamericana Ciudad de México and is currently earning a doctorate at the same university. She has participated in the Festival Internacional Cervantino in Guanajuato, Mexico, and in literary festivals in Montevideo, Bogota, Mexico City, and Madrid. She wrote the literary study *El decir de lo indecible: Los rodeos del deseo en la obra de Alejandra Pizarnik* and the poetry collection *Alimaña*. Her poems have appeared in *Asymptote* and the *Colorado Review*. Her favorite Uruguayan poets are Amanda Berenguer and Eduardo Milán. In English, she admires Ted Hughes and Ezra Pound.

"EL HOSKI" is the pseudonym of JOSÉ LUIS GADEA, born in Montevideo in 1988. He is a literature teacher and musician whose books include *Breve antología poética de Martín Uruguay Martínez*, written under the heteronym Martín Uruguay Martínez. El Hoski's poems have appeared in *Palabras Errantes*. He is a founder of Orientación Poesía, which brings poetry to Uruguayan high schools. The Uruguayan poet and lyricist Leo Maslíah is an influence, as are the Portuguese poet Fernando Pessoa and the American Walt Whitman.

LEONARDO LESCI was born in Rosario, Uruguay, in 1981. He currently lives in Colonia del Sacramento, where he teaches literature and literary theory. He has collaborated on various publications in Colonia, including the cultural magazine *U*, which published a chapbook of his poems, *Intervalo*. He is the author of the poetry collections *Genealogía del ocio* and *River Plate*. His poems have appeared in *Palabras Errantes*. His favorite Uruguayan poet is Marosa di Giorgio. He also counts Charles Baudelaire as an influence.

AGUSTÍN LUCAS was born in Montevideo in 1985. He is the author of three books: *Insectario*, *No todos los dedos son prensiles*, and *Club*. He also a professional soccer player who has played for teams in Argentina, Guatemala, Venezuela, and Uruguay and who has written frequently about the game. His poems have appeared in *Diagram*, *EIL: Escape into Life*, *spoKe*, *Blue Lyra Review*, and *The Collagist*. His favorite Uruguayan poets include Horacio Cavallo and Eduardo Curbelo. He also counts the Americans Jack Kerouac and Charles Bukowski as influences.

ELISA MASTROMATTEO was born in Montevideo in 1988. She is a student of psychology at the Universidad de la República. She is the author of *Tan simple como eso*, and her work was included in the anthology *Los hijos del fuego*. Her poems have appeared in *Prairie Schooner* and *Palabras Errantes*. The Uruguayan poet Idea Vilariño is her major influence, and she also enjoys the work of Alfredo Fressia.

ALEX PIPERNO was born in Montevideo in 1985. He is a writer and filmmaker. His books of poetry are *Los estándares de belleza en los pastizales*, *Sahara*, *Bagrejaponés*, *Maschwitz*, and *Confirmación del paraíso*. The poets who influenced him most are the Uruguayans Julio Inverso, Marosa di Giorgio, Manuel Barrios, and Santiago Márquez and the Chilean Juan Luis Martínez.

ALICIA PREZA was born in Montevideo in 1981. Her poetry collection is *El ojo de la lluvia*, and her poems have been published in *Palabras Errantes*. She is the cofounder of the Montevideo reading series La pluma azul. The Uruguayan poets who have influenced her include Marosa di Giorgio and Selva Casal. Her favorite English-language poet is Walt Whitman.

SEBASTIÁN RIVERO was born in Colonia del Sacramento, Uruguay, in 1978. He is a history teacher and a journalist writing about artistic, cultural, and historical events for national publications. He has published four books of poetry, including *Pequeños crímenes cotidianos* and *Respública*. His poems have appeared in *Asymptote* and *spoKe*. His favorite Uruguayan poets are Salvador Puig and Elías Uriarte. His other influences include Ezra Pound, Oliverio Girondo, Stéphane Mallarmé, Fernando Pessoa, and Constantine Cavafy.

JUAN MANUEL SÁNCHEZ was born in Montevideo in 1983. He is a student at the Universidad de la República. He teaches literature classes, writes literary reviews for *La Diaria*, and works in the Centro Cultural Castillo Pittamiglio. He is the author of the poetry collection *Para las focas*, and his poems appear in *Palabras Errantes*. His favorite Uruguayan poet is Roberto Genta Dorado, and he appreciates the American poets Walt Whitman and Edgar Allan Poe.

FABIÁN SEVERO was born in Artigas, Uruguay, in 1981. He is a literature teacher and conducts creative writing workshops. He is the author of the poetry collections *Noite nu norte*, *Viento de nadie*, and *NósOtros*. His poems appeared in *Poetry* and *Words without*

Borders. His favorite Uruguayan poet is Circe Maia, but his work is also influenced by César Vallejo and Fernando Pessoa.

PAULA SIMONETTI was born in Montevideo in 1989. She has a degree in literature from the Universidad de la República and is the author of the poetry collection *En la boca de los tristes.* She is an educator in shelters, working with children at risk and the homeless. Her poems have appeared in the *American Poetry Review*, *Notre Dame Review*, *spoKe*, *Modern Poetry in Translation*, and *Words without Borders.* Her favorite Uruguayan poets are Idea Vilariño, Ida Vitale, and Selva Casal. Other poets who have influenced her include César Vallejo, Juan Gelman, and Roque Dalton.

FRANCISCO TOMSICH was born in Rosario, Uruguay, in 1981. He is a visual artist, a musician, a writer, and the coauthor, with Horacio Cavallo, of the poetry collection *Sonetos a dos.* His poems have appeared in *Palabras Errantes.* His favorite Uruguayan poet is Álvaro Figueredo. His favorite poets in English include William Shakespeare, William Blake, Walt Whitman, Ezra Pound, and Charles Olson.

KAREN WILD DÍAZ was born in Montevideo in 1984. She studied at the Université Paris 8 and is now an assistant professor at the Universidad de la República. Her book of poetry *Anti-férula* will be published in English translation in the United States as *Anti-Ferule.* Her poems have appeared in the Argentine anthology *Hijas de diablo hijas de santo*, *Blue Lyra Review*, and *Copper Nickel.* Her favorite Uruguayan poet is Marosa di Giorgio. Other influences include Walt Whitman, Antonin Artaud, and Arthur Rimbaud.

Translators

DAN BELLM is the author of the poetry collections *One Hand on the Wheel*, *Buried Treasure*, and *Practice*, and he has translated book-length collections by the poets Pierre Reverdy, Jorge Esquinca, and Pura López Colomé. He teaches literary translation in the MFA program at Antioch University Los Angeles. His favorite poet in Spanish is Pablo Neruda; in English, his favorites are James Schuyler and Elizabeth Bishop.

DON BOGEN is the author of four books of poetry, including *An Algebra* and *Luster*. He is the Nathaniel Ropes Professor of English and Comparative Literature at the University of Cincinnati and poetry editor of the *Cincinnati Review*. His favorite poet in Spanish is Julio Martínez Mesanza and in English, William Butler Yeats.

GEOFFREY BROCK is author of *Voices Bright Flags*, editor of *The FSG Book of Twentieth-Century Italian Poetry*, and translator of Cesare Pavese's *Disaffections: Complete Poems, 1930–1950*. He teaches in the MFA program in creative writing and translation at the University of Arkansas. His favorite poets are César Vallejo in Spanish and Emily Dickinson in English.

JONA COLSON's poetry has appeared in *Subtropics*, *Prairie Schooner*, the *Southern Review*, and *Crab Orchard Review*. He is an assistant professor at Montgomery College in Maryland. In Spanish, his favorite poet is Pablo Neruda; in English, Anne Sexton.

KEITH EKISS is the author of the poetry collection *Pima Road Notebook* and the translator of *The Fire's Journey* by the Costa Rican poet Eunice Odio. He was a Jones Lecturer in Poetry at Stanford University. His favorite poets are Federico García Lorca in Spanish and Elizabeth Bishop in English.

ADAM GIANNELLI is a poet and the translator of prose poems by Marosa di Giorgio that were published in English as *Diadem* in 2012. He is a doctoral candidate in literature and creative writing at the University of Utah. His favorite poet in Spanish is Alejandra Pizarnik; in English, Emily Dickinson.

KEVIN GONZÁLEZ is the author of the poetry collection *Cultural Studies*. He is the editor of *jubilat* and coeditor of *The New Census: An Anthology of Contemporary American Poetry*. He teaches creative writing at Carnegie Mellon University. His favorite poet in Spanish is Juan Antonio Corretjer; in English, Larry Levis.

CATHERINE JAGOE is the author of the poetry book *Casting Off*. Her translations include the Argentine novel *My Name Is Light* by Elsa Osorio, which won the Amnesty International Award for Fiction, and *That Bringas Woman* by Benito Pérez Galdós. Her favorite poet is Federico García Lorca in Spanish and in English, Seamus Heaney.

JESSE LEE KERCHEVAL, the Zona Gale Professor of English at the University of Wisconsin, is the author of thirteen books, including the bilingual collection of her poems *Extranjera / Stranger*. Her translations include *The Invisible Bridge / El puente invisible: Selected Poems of Circe Maia*. She is the editor of *América invertida*. Her favorite poet in Spanish is Circe Maia; in English, Walt Whitman.

JULIA LEVERONE is a poet and translator. She teaches in North Texas, where she is writing her doctoral dissertation in comparative literature for Washington University in St. Louis. Julia is the editor of *Sakura Review*. Her translations of Francisco "Paco" Urondo's poetry have appeared in the *Brooklyn Rail*, *Witness*, *Massachusetts Review*, *Poetry International*, and *Tupelo Quarterly*. Her favorite poet in Spanish is Dulce María Loynaz; in English, Elizabeth Bishop.

VICENTE MARCOS LÓPEZ ABAD, born in Valencia, Spain, is a bilingual poet and doctoral candidate in Spanish literature with a minor in creative writing at the University of Wisconsin–Madison. His first poetry collection, *Divertimiento*, is forthcoming from Editorial Baile del Sol in Spain. His poems have appeared in *PEN International*, *Poetic Republic*, *Vulture*, and *Turia*. His favorite poet in Spanish is César Vallejo and in English, Seamus Heaney.

ERICA MENA is a poet, translator, and book artist. Her book-length poem *Featherbone* is available from Ricochet Editions. Her translations include the Argentine graphic novel *The Eternaut* by Héctor Germán Oesterheld and Francisco Solano López. She is the executive director of the American Literary Translators Association and the founding editor of Anomalous Press. Pablo Neruda is her favorite poet in Spanish and Rosmarie Waldrop her favorite in English.

ORLANDO RICARDO MENES is the author of five poetry books, most recently *Heresies*. His translations include *My Heart Flooded with Water: Selected Poems by Alfonsina Storni*. He teaches in the creative writing program at the University of Notre Dame and is the poetry editor of the *Notre Dame Review*. His favorite Spanish-language poet is César Vallejo. Derek Walcott is his favorite in English.

SETH MICHELSON is the author of four collections of poetry, including *Eyes Like Broken Windows*, and the translator of *Roly Poly* by Victoria Estol, whose work he also translated for this anthology. He is an assistant professor of Spanish at Washington and Lee University. In Spanish, his favorite poet is Juan Gelman; in English, Thomas Lux and Adrienne Rich.

ANNA ROSENWONG is a translator, editor, poet, and educator. Her translations include Rocío Cerón's *Diorama* (winner of the 2015 Best Translated Book Award), José Eugenio Sánchez's *Suite Prelude A / H1N1*, and Sánchez's forthcoming *Climax with Double Cheese*. Her poetry chapbook is *By Way of Explanation*. Her literary and scholarly work has been featured in *World Literature Today*, *Kenyon Review*, *Translation Studies*, *St. Petersburg Review*, *Pool*, and elsewhere. Her favorite poet in Spanish is José Eugenio Sánchez; in English, Cole Swensen.

RON PAUL SALUTSKY is the author of the poetry collection *Romeo Bones* and a member of the arts and humanities faculty at Southern Regional Technical College in Thomasville, Georgia. His translation of Karen Wild Díaz's *Anti-Ferule* was published by Toad Press. His favorite Spanish-language poets are Alejandra Pizarnik, Marosa di Giorgio, and the Costa Rican poet Alfredo Trejos, whose work he translates.

CHRISTOPHER SCHAFENACKER is a poet and translator of works by the Uruguayan writers Olga Leiva and Inés Bortagaray, among others. He is a doctoral student in comparative literature at the University of Massachusetts Amherst. His favorite poets are Federico García Lorca in Spanish and Martín Espada in English.

CINDY SCHUSTER is a poet and translator of Latin American writers. She cotranslated *Cubana: Contemporary Fiction by Cuban Women.* She holds a doctorate in Spanish from the University of California, Irvine, and was a board member of the American Literary Translators Association. Her favorite poet in Spanish is Alejandra Pizarnik. Frank O'Hara is her favorite in English.

LAUREN SHAPIRO is the author of the poetry collection *Easy Math.* She has translated poetry and fiction from Italian, Spanish, Vietnamese, and Arabic into English. She teaches in the creative writing program at Carnegie Mellon University. Her favorite poet in Spanish is Pablo Neruda. In English, she enjoys Emily Dickinson and Kenneth Koch.

MARK STATMAN is the author of the poetry collection *A Map of the Winds* and the translator of *Black Tulips: The Selected Poems of José María Hinojosa.* With Pablo Medina, he translated *Poet in New York* by Frederico García Lorca. His translation of *Never Made in America: Selected Poems in Translation* by Martín Barea Mattos will be published by Lavender Ink in 2017. He is an associate professor of literary studies at Eugene Lang College of Liberal Arts at the New School. His favorite Spanish-language poets include Jorge Luis Borges and Mario Benedetti. In English, he admires William Carlos Williams and Elizabeth Bishop.